WORKING IN JAILS AND PRISONS

BECOMING PART OF THE TEAM

By Daniel J. Bayse

Celebrating Our 125th Anniversary
American Correctional Association
4380 Forbes Boulevard
Lanham, MD 20706

Bobbie L. Huskey, President
James A. Gondles, Jr., Executive Director
Karen L. Kushner, Director, Communications and Publications
Alice Fins, Publications Managing Editor
Jill Furniss, Associate Editor
Kevin Ogburn, Production Editor and Designer
Capitol Communication Systems, Inc., Cover Design

This publication may be ordered from:
American Correctional Association
4380 Forbes Boulevard
Lanham, MD 20706
1-800-825-BOOK

Library of Congress Cataloging-in-Publication Data

Bayse, Daniel J. (Daniel Justin)
Working in jails and prisons : becoming part of the team / Daniel J. Bayse.
p. cm
"Companion to the book: Helping hands"—Acknowledgments.
Includes bibliographical references.
ISBN 1-56991-021-9
1. Correctional personnel—Training of—United States.
2. Correctional psychology—United States. 3. Criminal behavior—United States. 4. Criminal psychology—United States. I. Bayse, Daniel J. (Daniel Justin). Helping hands. II. Title.
HV9470.B39   1995
365'.023'73—dc20   95-8358
                                                            CIP

Contents

Chapter 1: Yesterday's and Today's Crime, Punishment, and Corrections

Chapter 2: Understanding the Criminal Personality

Chapter 3: Inmates: Our Reason for Working

Chapter 4: Effective Ways to Work with Inmates

Chapter 5: Avoiding the Pitfalls

Foreword

People who work in correctional facilities are like players on a team. The "players" include: correctional officers, administrative and management personnel, support staff (food service, maintenance, and clerical), professional specialists, probation and parole officers, and volunteers. Each has a different role. The "team" has many players, but all should be working toward the same goal—rehabilitating the offender. At times, achieving this goal may seem impossible, especially considering the crowded conditions of facilities and the stress that accompanies many of these jobs. By accepting your membership as a team player, you are taking your first step.

Daniel Bayse wrote *Working in Jails and Prisons: Becoming Part of the Team* to help correctional workers understand the system in which they work (or will be working) and how, by cooperating with other employees as a team, they can prepare inmates to be contributing members of society. Written on a personal level, Bayse's book contains stories and practical advice that reflect his vast experience in the correctional system. This book provides not only a look inside the correctional facility, but inside the mind of the criminal, as well. As Bayse explains, "Inmates have lots of time on their hands, and they are constantly watching for employees who they feel would be susceptible to manipulation." The more a correctional worker knows about what to expect from inmates, the better prepared that person will be.

In *Working in Jails and Prisons*, Bayse reminds us that rehabilitation is possible, but "it takes the coordinated efforts of the entire team to help inmates realize that they have the power to change." Good luck in your correctional career—it can have multiple rewards.

James A. Gondles, Jr.
Executive Director
American Correctional Association

Dedication

Becoming a team member always requires dedicated coaches. This book is dedicated to five professionals who helped me change from a person who believed that "nothing works" into someone who now realizes that inmate rehabilitation is possible when everyone works together as a team: J. Michael Burns, Ed.D.; R. Carrol Hammack, Ph.D.; Scot M. Allgood, Ph.D.; Hugh H. Donnan, Ph.D.; and John C. Moracco, Ph.D.

Acknowledgments

This book was designed to be a companion to the book *Helping Hands: A Handbook for Volunteers in Prisons and Jails* (Bayse 1993). It was written with the help of many people. Besides the authors of the many employee training materials, books, journal articles, research projects, and volunteer manuals used as resources for this book, there are many others who made special contributions. My appreciation goes to the state and federal officials who responded to my request for information about their staff training programs.

Appreciation is expressed to Morris L. Thigpen, director, National Institute of Corrections, for his guidance, which helped make this book possible.

The staff of the Alabama Department of Corrections are acknowledged for their many contributions. Paul H. Van Wyk, Ph.D., director of mental health services, and Pamela C. Van Wyk, director of the special programs unit for sex offenders at the Bullock County Correctional Facility, Union Springs, Alabama, spent many hours editing rough drafts, providing valuable insights into the needs of inmates, and giving encouragement.

Merle R. Friesen, Ed.D., director of treatment, Alabama Department of Corrections, and Deputy Warden Ray Russell of the Tutwiler Prison for Women in Alabama also provided insight and encouragement. Lee County, Alabama, Circuit Court Judge James Gullege provided insight into the court process. Master Trooper H. W. English, Virginia State Police, provided copies of some of Virginia's laws. Harry K. Singletary, Jr., secretary, Florida Department of Corrections, furnished a treatise on the development of effective careers in corrections.

The assistance of Kathleen M. Hawk, director, Federal Bureau of Prisons, is also appreciated; as is that of Director Jean-Paul Bélanger, corporate classification and staffing, and Aldean Andersen, acting chief, correspondence control, Correctional Service of Canada.

The following individuals provided copies of their state's or agency's training materials: Larry R. Meachum, former director, Connecticut Department of Corrections; Howard A. Peters III, former director, Illinois Department of Corrections; Larry E. DuBois, commissioner; and Ralph Keith, director of training and evaluation, Massachusetts Department of Correction; and Kenneth L. McGinnis, director, Michigan Department of Corrections.

Also to be thanked are the following individuals: Dora B. Schiro, director, Missouri Department of Corrections; Daniel L. Stieneke, director, Office of Staff Development and Training, North Carolina Department of Correction; Larry A. Fields, director, Oklahoma Department of Corrections; Frank A. Hall, director, Oregon Department of Corrections; Randy L. Pollock, associate director of training services, and Rick Heldibridle, SCI Cresson, Pennsylvania Department of Corrections; and Art Mosley, assistant director, personnel and training, Texas Department of Criminal Justice.

I acknowledge the officials who provided materials that are used in this book and in *Helping Hands*: Lynn Doggett, volunteer services program coordinator, Arkansas Department of Corrections; Gary Stotts, Kansas' secretary of corrections; Nancy Williams, director, chaplaincy and volunteer services, Maryland Division of Correction; William L. Schnitzer, acting director, volunteer services coordinator, New York Department of Correctional Services; Walter D. Thieszen, chief of program services, Division of Adult Institutions, Wisconsin Department of Corrections; and Deputy Warden Nola Cole, Wyoming Women's Center of Corrections.

—*Daniel J. Bayse*, Ed.S., LPC, CFLE

Introduction

Correctional facilities need good staff members. Prisons and jails are bulging at the seams. Although building new and larger facilities to hold more inmates is one way to handle the problem, it is only a temporary fix. Inmates serve their sentences and are released, but many return to prison. To reduce recidivism, inmates need to be rehabilitated while they are incarcerated.

Accomplishing this task takes the coordinated effort of the whole correctional team: administration, security, and the entire support staff. The entire correctional team giving of themselves can help turn inmates into productive members of society. When the strong make sacrifices to help the weaker members of society, society as a whole is strengthened.

Inmates live with other inmates. Over time, many begin accepting the attitudes, values, and behavior patterns of the more hardened inmates and become career criminals. Effective staff members can help stop this process by being positive role models for inmates. Staff members can prove to inmates that the whole world is not self-centered. By their ability to be as "tough as nails" whenever necessary and still treat the inmate with respect, they show inmates that people in the system do actually care. Even hardened criminals respond to concern and respect.

It takes a special person to work with inmates. Behind the steel bars are murderers, robbers, rapists, drug dealers, extortionists, swindlers, child molesters, and people who are guilty of other equally ugly crimes. Effective prison and jail workers see beyond the crime to the basic value of the individual. What makes these correctional people special is their belief in an individual's ability to change and the realization that a lifetime of dysfunction is not transformed overnight.

This book is designed to help people who seek to work inside correctional facilities to become team workers. There is no place inside a prison or jail for a "lone ranger." The person who plows the ground or plants the seeds may not be the one who reaps the crop. Each is equally important if the harvest is to be complete. Corrections work is much the same. Even though some jobs have more prestigious titles, each person who works within the system has a vital role. Each is part of the inmate's rehabilitation process.

Prisons and jails need workers who will help, not cause problems. Although most correctional workers have a genuine desire to help, many cause problems simply because they do not understand how the average inmate thinks, or they drop their guard only for a moment and do something that harms themselves and others. This book is designed to help new employees gain a knowledge of inmates and correctional systems. It even has a glossary to help you understand some prison slang.

Working in an environment where freedom is restrained is challenging. Working with a system that is sometimes inflexible and with inmates who seem angry at the whole world (including you) is frustrating. But, it can also be rewarding. This author cannot think of a more rewarding experience than helping inmates abandon their criminal ways and begin working toward becoming worthwhile members of society. That is what corrections is all about.

Yesterday's and Today's Crime, Punishment, and Corrections

The Beginning of Crime

Crime is as old as humans themselves. In fact, the biblical account of the first couple on earth reveals that they possessed criminal thought patterns.

In this story, Eve met a con-artist with a long record of trying to overthrow the government. This master manipulator skillfully persuaded her to bypass the posted signs, trespass on private property, and steal and eat fruit. She then took some fruit home to her husband. Adam, knowing it was stolen, willingly took the fruit and ate it. They were caught and questioned. Like most criminals, instead of accepting responsibility, they tried to blame someone else. Adam and Eve became the first of many to use the excuse "The devil made me do it." The truth is that this crime, like *all* crimes, consisted of four steps:

1. They saw something they wanted but had no right to have.

2. They declared that neither God nor society had any right to tell them to control their urges.

3. They abused their power when they took or did it.

4. When they did, they earned the penalty prescribed by the law for their crime.

Adam and Eve, like most criminals, did not think they would be caught. The penalty they earned was more than they expected. They were the first of many to learn about the lifelong stigma of being convicted criminals.

Just as it is today, when crime became part of their lives, their entire world changed. Peaceful living was replaced with fear. Work became a pain. Honesty and openness were replaced with lies and secrecy. A marriage made in heaven itself became a continuing power struggle to determine who would rule the family. Both their son and grandson became murderers. Their descendants became the first of many generations to copy family attitudes, values, and behavior patterns.

With each passing generation the chain of criminality has become stronger. Since 1985, according to the Department of Justice's *National Update* (1992), at least one-in-four American families has been the victim of serious crimes each year. Prison populations have more than doubled in the past ten years. In fact, the Department of Justice (May 1993; August 1993) figures show that by the end of 1992, a record 1.33 million inmates were housed in United States prisons and jails. Figures released by the Justice Department (1994) indicate that 71 percent of the women and 80 percent of the men admitted into state prisons had criminal histories. An additional 2.7 million people were on probation (Greenfeld 1992). It has become so bad that at the end of 1990, one out of every forty-three adults in the United States was under correctional supervision (Jankowski 1992). Prisons and jails are bulging beyond capacity. Unfortunately, there is no relief in sight.

Clearly, something has to be done. Since most crime is done by repeat offenders, effective correctional workers are an important part of that "something."

Early Attempts to Control Crime

Ancient tribes quickly learned that the selfish and evil actions of a few required them to band together for their own protection. Crimes that affected the community or angered the gods were considered the most serious (e.g., employing witchcraft, spying, violating of tribal taboos, and others). The guilty were usually tortured to death. Early forms of punishment included: stoning, being sealed inside bags with poisonous snakes, being fed to wild animals, or being crucified. Those not executed were frequently ostracized and banned from the community.

Originally, crime committed by one individual against another was not considered a community matter. These types of crimes were settled under the doctrine of *lex talionis*, "an eye for an eye and a tooth for a tooth." The victim, or the victim's family, was responsible for catching and punishing the criminal. When the perpetrator was caught, the victim or a family member inflicted the original injury on the guilty party. Accidents were not excused.

In *The Story of Punishment*, Barnes (1972) says that the literalness of this method was astonishing. For example, a man who killed another while falling out of a tree was himself killed when the victim's relative jumped out of a tree onto him. Retaliatory wounds were matched as closely as possible to the damage done to the victim. For example, a victim who received a two-inch knife wound to the stomach was required to stab the guilty party's stomach and administer a two-inch knife wound.

This system was ineffective. Angry victims frequently demanded much harsher penalties than they were allowed to inflict. Also, many guilty parties did not willingly submit to this process. They would flee or seek protection from their family and friends. This produced feuds between clans that would sometimes last for generations.

There was another problem. People discovered that revenge could be a very painful experience. Most people do not want the responsibility of personally executing a criminal, even if he or she had been a victim earlier.

The Evolution of Criminal Justice

In *A History of Corrections*, Schmalleger (1986) shows that people began to look to their leaders for justice. Punishment by revenge was replaced by a system of fines designed to pay the victims for the harm done to them. Those found guilty of inflicting personal injuries paid higher fines than those convicted of property offenses. These fines were used to pay the victims for their losses.

Historian Hibbert (1978) says that by the seventh century, the amount paid in each case was carefully stipulated. Each body part had a specific value. The loss of an eye cost one amount, a toenail a lesser amount. Executions were reserved for those found guilty of serious crimes such as treason or murder, or sexual perversion.

Deciding who was telling the truth was, and still is, a problem. Early civilizations frequently used torture to decide the truthfulness of testimony and to gain confessions. Superstition held that the gods would either protect the innocent from harm or would produce supernatural healing. Thus, the accused were required to walk through fire, place their hands in boiling water, endure a hot sword on their tongues, or other equally gruesome "tests." If they were not hurt, or if the wound healed quickly, they were considered to be telling the truth. If not, they were considered liars and were executed. Confessions given during these tortures were accepted and frequently used as justification for executing the accused.

During the Middle Ages, people began asking twelve reputable neighbors known as "compurgators" to listen to testimony of both sides and make decisions. Barnes (1972) says that the number twelve was selected because of its significance in both the Old and New Testaments of the Bible. This system evolved into the present-day trial by jury.

Courts of law came into existence with the establishment of central governments. Law books were written by the leaders of these governments. Kings appointed magistrates and judges to hear cases and render judgments.

In 1100 A.D., England's King Henry I declared all criminal acts violations of the "King's peace." Fines went into the king's treasury to pay for the "damage" done to the kingdom. Victims were no longer paid for their losses. Instead, they became witnesses for the government and bystanders in the whole judicial process. The courts gained complete control of all sentencing—from fines to executions.

Courts began trying to understand why criminals chose to break the law. Punishments were designed to be so awful that the criminal, and those watching, would stop committing crimes.

Thus, punishment was inflicted in the form of public hangings, beheadings, using dunking chairs and torture chambers, burnings, and other equally gruesome public executions. Also common were public beatings, brandings, and various other forms of mutilation. For example, thieves might have a hand cut off. To make them unattractive, women caught in adultery lost an ear or a nose. People caught cursing had holes drilled in their tongue. If not executed, rapists were frequently castrated. Requiring people to spend hours in the stocks was popular for a time. To add to the offender's shame, the public was invited to pelt the person with rotten food, rocks, or whatever else they could find. Many offenders died as a result.

Although public torture is no longer legal, this basic legal system that began in England is still in use today. Only the local, state, or federal government can charge an individual in a criminal case. Victims are witnesses. Only courts can give sentences, and fines are the property of the government. Offenders, when sentenced, are housed in government-operated prisons and jails. Lawmakers and the public still hope that the sentences imposed will deter crime.

The Evolution of Jails and Prisons

Until about 300 years ago jails were used primarily to hold people until a trial could be arranged. Large prisons were not needed because once trials were over, criminals received their punishment immediately. The death penalty, when given, was usually carried out by the end of the day.

Early reformers suggested that moving offenders into prison colonies would help reduce crime. Some prison colonies were little more than slave camps. Others gave offenders another chance, sending them to remote areas, such as Siberia and Australia. Some were even brought to America. Once in America, convicted criminals could earn their freedom by working as servants for a specified period.

Times changed and societies grew. People began noticing that punishment designed to humiliate and torture did little to deter crime. Banishment from one community, or even into a prison penal colony, simply moved the problem from one place to another.

In the sixteenth century, European leaders started gathering criminals and placing them in large workhouses. Most had been arrested for vagrancy. To "cure" their laziness, inmates were forced to spend long hours at hard labor. There were no established standards then, and conditions in these privately run institutions were horrible. Rules were enforced with whips and other harsh punishments. Inmates had to pay for their room and board. Many were forced to remain after their sentences had expired simply because workhouse salaries did not cover imprisonment costs. Forced prison labor created a source of inexpensive merchandise. Prisons made handsome profits selling the products of the inmates' labor.

The 1700s marked a period of reform in both Europe and America. In 1704, Pope Clement XI created the first "training school" for delinquent boys. The Pope felt that doing hard work while learning discipline would produce repentance. This, in turn, was supposed to help change the delinquent into a productive citizen. It worked, and the basic system that he started is still in use today.

In 1773, Belgium created a prison system that provided separate quarters for men, women, and children. Before this, all offenders, including children, were frequently housed in the same rooms. Rehabilitation efforts replaced the system of employing harsh punishments and profiting from inmates' work. Volunteers taught vocational skills.

In 1790, Philadelphia Quakers created penitentiaries—places to do penance for one's crime. Inmates were placed in solitary cells with nothing but a Bible. The Quakers believed that inmates could be rehabilitated if they were given enough time to reflect on their evil actions. It did not work; many inmates thus confined went insane.

Quakers in New York tried a different approach. Inmates were housed in dormitory-type rooms segregated by sex and the seriousness of their crimes. Silence was enforced. Inmates spent long hours in hard labor. Inmates who refused to obey the rules were placed in solitary confinement for short periods of time. Inmates were taught trades. Men learned shoemaking, weaving, tailoring, and woodworking. Women learned spinning, washing, and sewing. Volunteers were an important part of the correctional team. Each weekend they came into the prison to teach the Bible and moral values. Inmates eagerly awaited the volunteers' arrival because it was their only contact with the outside world. Leaders from around the world came to study and duplicate the New York Quakers' approach to corrections.

Many reforms occurred in the 1800s. Hibbert (1978) says that in 1833 Tennessee began giving inmates time off for good behavior. Vermont began allowing well-behaved inmates to have tobacco, letters, and visitors. In 1842, Georgia began using a system of rewards and punishments. During this time, Massachusetts began allowing education other than religious instruction. Connecticut prisons instituted an honor system among inmates. With each reform, the penitentiary, with its focus on the rehabilitation of inmates, became a more permanent part of the criminal justice system.

Volunteers Are an Important Part of the Team

Ideas born through volunteers have been the source of many of the improvements that have become the heart of modern day corrections. Unfortunately, volunteers, like all workers, sometimes do cause problems. However, benefits provided by volunteers often can far outweigh the costs.

In *Elizabeth Fry: Quaker Heroine*, Whitney (1936) describes a cold January morning in 1813 when two women stepped out of their carriage and walked into London's Newgate prison. Their reaction to what they saw helped to start a prison reform movement that is still active today.

Outside, the huge buildings appeared orderly and beautiful. Inside, Elizabeth Fry was greeted with the stench of squalor. Hundreds of women, reduced to the level of animals by the living conditions, pressed their bodies against the bars hoping for attention. The prison had no beds, windows, or heat; few sanitary facilities; and little ventilation. Except for the ones wealthy enough to purchase straw or lucky enough to get a hammock, inmates slept on dirty, wooden floors. Adequate clothing was a luxury.

The two volunteers worked diligently to ease some of the suffering. They comforted inmates and provided clothing for naked babies. Sick inmates were given thick bedding of clean, fresh straw.

Fry could not get the sights and smells out of her mind. She became obsessed with prison reform. With the help of British nobility, she founded the Society for the Reformation of Prison Discipline. The modern prison-volunteer movement had begun. Volunteers became the unofficial watchdogs of the prison systems.

Other reformers followed. In 1841, John Augustus, a volunteer from Boston, introduced the practice of placing convicted criminals under the supervision of the community instead of prison authorities. Later, he became the nation's first probation officer. In the mid-1800s, the Philadelphia Society for Alleviating the Misery of Public Prisons started a program that supervised newly released inmates. This was the beginning of the modern parole system.

By the mid-twentieth century, prison systems began replacing volunteer workers with professionals: counselors, social workers, psychologists, teachers, and chaplains. As a result, in many systems, volunteers were considered unnecessary and were no longer welcome within the gates.

Today, prison officials are rediscovering what the Quakers learned two centuries ago. Volunteers are more than simply a way to stretch budgets. Inmates need role models from the free world if they are going to make it on the outside when they are released. Too often correctional officials cannot provide that role model because they may be seen as part of the system.

It takes training and experience for anyone to become an effective member of a team. New volunteers are just as inexperienced and make some of the same types of mistakes as new employees. The American Correctional Association has a companion book to this one, *Helping Hands: A Handbook for Volunteers in Prisons and Jails*. It is designed to help volunteers get off to a good start. You can continue the process by giving new volunteers the same type of support and encouragement as you would provide for a new employee.

Remember, volunteers come to correctional facilities on their own time, and at their own expense. Their only reward is the feeling of pride that they get when they have successfully given of themselves to help the weaker members of society out of their predicaments. By treating them with respect and taking the time to help them become part of the team, you and your facility will reap the rewards.

Today's Criminal Justice System

A criminal's road to jail and/or prison begins when a crime is committed. Frequently, charges are filed when a citizen swears out a warrant for arrest. If the crime is witnessed by the police, the criminal may be arrested on the spot. If not, the police will conduct an investigation before placing charges.

In any case, charges cannot be filed without probable cause. Probable cause is the amount of evidence that is required to convince an ordinary person that the suspect is *probably* the one who broke the law. Once the charges are placed, the case can move into a court of law.

Usually, things that are against the law in one state are against the law in other states. However, there are differences among systems. If you are transferring from one system to another, take the time and effort to learn about the law and the rules in your new jurisdiction. Each governing body (federal, state, county, or local) creates the wording of the laws in its jurisdiction. Consequently, the same crime may be called various names in different states (e.g., vehicular homicide may be called murder or manslaughter). The same crime may also be considered more serious in one state than in another. For example, in Alabama, shoplifting $225 worth of property from a store would be prosecuted as a misdemeanor, "Theft of Property in the Third Degree" (Title 13-A-8-5); in Virginia, it would be prosecuted as a felony, "Grand Larceny" (Title 18.2-103).

Laws that include prison or jail sentences are usually divided into two broad categories: misdemeanors and felonies. These categories determine the maximum sentences that can be imposed for the crime. They also determine the type of court procedure that will be used during the trial. Conviction in either category results in offenders having a criminal record.

Misdemeanors

Misdemeanors are less serious than felonies. Examples of misdemeanors could include: shoplifting of a candy bar, slapping someone with one's hand, or having a small amount of illegal drugs. If convicted, the maximum penalty for a misdemeanor is spending time in the local jail and/or paying a fine. The limits are set by the state legislatures. Many states set the limit at a $1,000 fine and a year in jail.

Misdemeanors are usually tried in a local court by a judge. These courts may be called the district, city, police, or county court. The trials are usually somewhat informal. There may or may not be attorneys present. Frequently, the people involved in the trial stand in front of the judge to testify. Once the evidence is heard, the judge renders a verdict. If found guilty, the accused has the right to appeal the case to a higher court.

Felonies

Examples of felonies include: murder, rape, robbery, and sale of drugs. Those convicted of felonies may receive very heavy fines and/or many years in a state or federal penitentiary. "Capital" felonies, such as capital murder, are those crimes that carry the death penalty. Because the penalties are so severe, the law requires that additional steps be taken before a person can be tried, convicted, and sentenced.

In almost all cases, after the accused is arrested, police officials conduct the process of fingerprinting and photographing the arrestee. A magistrate or judge determines (1) if the accused can be released on bond until the trial and (2) if he or she needs to have an attorney appointed to represent him or her during the court proceedings.

Some states require the accused to appear at a preliminary hearing. The preliminary hearing is not a trial; it is a quick review of the evidence by a district or local judge to see if there is enough "probable cause" to support the charge. If there is probable cause, the accused proceeds to the next step. Usually, this is either to the grand jury or, in some states, to trial.

Hearings before grand juries are designed to determine if there is enough evidence to support the charges. Since they do not determine guilt, generally, the accused does not testify and usually is not present. Some prosecutions begin at this stage. Formal charges may be filed after the grand jury delivers an indictment against the accused.

The actual trial comes next. Although the name of the court varies among states, it is usually called the Circuit Court, Superior Court, or Court of Common Pleas. In New York it is called the Supreme Court. At the trial, the defendant has three choices: (1) plead guilty or no contest, and hope for mercy, (2) plea bargain for reduced charges or the best sentence possible, or (3) plead "not guilty" and take his or her chances before the judge and/or jury.

A plea of "not guilty" is not considered a lie, even if the defendant is, in fact, guilty. It simply means that the defendant wants the case to be tried. Normally, a jury hears the evidence. At the trial, each side presents its evidence and guilt is determined.

A finding of "guilty" does not mean that the evidence was 100 percent conclusive. It only means that the evidence was strong enough for the jury and/or judge to believe "beyond a reasonable doubt" that the accused actually committed the crime.

A finding of "not guilty" does not mean the person is not guilty. Legally, people are innocent until proven guilty. The finding may mean that the prosecution failed to prove its case. It also could mean that the defense created enough doubt so that a guilty verdict could not be supported.

If found not guilty, the accused goes free. He or she cannot be tried again on the same charge in the same jurisdiction, even if additional evidence is found later. If found guilty, a sentence is imposed. Any conviction carries with it the right to appeal the case to a higher court. Sometimes, even the U.S. Supreme Court will agree to hear the appeal. An appeal can be a long and drawn-out process that takes many years.

Appellate courts never declare convicted offenders not guilty. Instead, they determine if the guilty verdict should be overturned because the evidence did not support the verdict or if some procedural error occurred during the trial. If overturned, the case would go back to the trial court. Sometimes, only the sentence is reconsidered. Other times, the appeals court may order a new trial. If the prosecutor decides not to retry the case, the defendant goes free.

This is not a perfect system, and mistakes do happen. However, the system is designed to set a guilty person free rather than convict an innocent person. These safeguards make it rare for an innocent person to be convicted and sent to prison.

Differences Between Jails and Prisons

Jails

In most jurisdictions, jails are operated by the local sheriff and his or her staff. Since jails are criminals' first stop, cells must accommodate everyone from drunks to mass murderers. Security must be tight. Inmates usually do not stay in jail very long.

Jails come in many different sizes and shapes. The Justice Department (1992) figures show that 80 percent of the nation's 4,000 jails hold fewer than fifty inmates. Others are large facilities that house more than 3,000 inmates. Treatment facilities in jails range from nonexistent to complete rehabilitation and education.

Unlike what happens in prisons, many inmates in jail have never been convicted of a crime. Many are accused of crimes and are waiting to be released on bond. Others, unable to post bond, are waiting for their trial dates. Some have been found guilty and are awaiting sentencing. Other inmates may be convicted felons waiting for transfer to a state prison, a process which can take months. Still others have been convicted of a misdemeanor and are serving their sentences, which can range from a few hours to months.

Being held in jail is very unsettling. So is waiting to be transferred to prison. Suicide attempts are common. Moods of jail inmates range from remorse and repentance to anger and hostility.

State Prison Systems

Prisons hold convicted felons. Most prisons are located in remote areas that are not served by public transportation. Each is part of a unified system operated under the authority of an agency, usually known as the department of corrections. They function with a strict chain of command. Depending on the state, the head of the state prison system is known as the commissioner, director, or secretary. He or she will have a variety of assistants who direct different parts of the prison system. Most states employ a volunteer coordinator to direct the activities of the volunteers within the system.

Each prison has a warden or superintendent who is in charge of the prison's overall operation. Both inmates and staff answer to the warden or superintendent. Next in the line of command is the deputy warden, assistant warden, or assistant superintendent. After this are uniformed security staff and civilian employees.

Security staff (known as correctional officers, not guards) form the backbone of the prison. They are responsible for maintaining law and order within the system. Everyone who works inside a correctional facility should cooperate with the security staff and treat them with respect. Inmates watch closely to see how much respect the support staff gives to the security staff's authority.

Civilian employees make up the rest of the staff. These include people who work in administration, treatment, classification, mental health, health care, education, workshops, maintenance, food services, and the chapel. Volunteers usually work under the supervision of the support staff.

The Federal Prison System

The Federal Bureau of Prisons (BOP) was established in 1930 by Congress. It is responsible for the safekeeping, caring, protecting, instructing, and disciplining of all persons charged or convicted of offenses against the United States. To carry out its responsibilities, the Federal Bureau of Prisons has established seventy-one correctional institutions ranging from penitentiaries to prison camps.

Instead of jails, the Federal Bureau of Prisons has seven Metropolitan Correctional Centers. They are designed for offenders serving short sentences or awaiting trial or sentencing. Inmates who require medical, surgical, or psychiatric care may be sent to one of four Federal Medical Centers.

Like state prisons, each federal prison is headed by a warden. The warden is responsible for the safe, secure, and smooth operation of the institution. The chain of command in the federal system is similar to that of most state prison systems.

Names and Titles

The most visible employees are the correctional officers. They *are not* guards and may be highly insulted if referred to as such. Today's correctional officers are trained professionals who are considered part of the team. Their job can be very stressful. They listen to inmates complain eight hours a day; inmates resent them. One of the correctional officer's primary responsibilities is helping inmates learn that breaking a rule is asking for the penalty that follows. This is a skill inmates must learn if they are to make it on the outside when they are released.

One of the most important things a new employee can do to be accepted is to address jail and prison personnel by their titles. Not only does it show respect, but it demonstrates that the employee wants to be part of the system.

The proper way to address a correctional officer is "officer" followed by his or her last name. Some jails use the title of "deputy." Others simply call the officer by his or her last name. Uniformed supervisors are called by their title (e.g., Sergeant Smith, Lieutenant Jones, or Captain Doe). The uniforms worn by staff have different insignia that designate their unique rank. Everyone working within an institution should learn to recognize the uniform and the insignia. They should show their respect by using the proper titles when addressing staff.

Each correctional facility is different. Most tend to be formal and people are addressed by their titles, or they use Mr. or Ms. before their last names. Medical doctors and those with doctorate degrees are known as "doctor." Many institutions discourage staff from calling inmates by their first name. If in doubt about what titles to use, employees should ask their supervisor what the policy is at that particular institution. It is better to ask than be embarrassed later.

Classification in Jails and Prisons

One way correctional officials try to manage inmates is by classifying them. The most dangerous criminals are placed in maximum security. They usually have long sentences and/or a history of violence. Movement within maximum security institutions is often restricted and monitored closely by security staff. Walls and fences inside the prison keep inmates apart. Activities are usually limited to small groups. These prisons have strict rules.

Medium security prisons house inmates who can usually abide by the rules, as long as they stay inside the prison. The security around the outside edge of the prison complex is very tight. Inside, inmates may have some freedom of movement.

Inmates with low risk factors are housed in minimum security prisons, work release programs, and community-based centers.

Security First, Programs Second

The primary responsibility of correctional facilities is to maintain security. A secondary function is to help inmates successfully reenter family life and society on release.

Prisons are harsh places. About 60 percent of the 1991 prison population consisted of violent offenders or people who had a history of violent crimes (Greenfeld 1992). Living in this harsh environment has an effect on inmates. Some will respond with hostility toward staff or other inmates, fear, or even emotional withdrawal. Others use manipulation and con games to get their own way.

People entering prison or jail for the first time are frequently surprised by the friendliness of inmates. Although many are very nice, looks can be deceiving. Many inmates use their "Sunday manners" around staff members. Underneath the friendly smile can also be a dangerous con-artist who can fool even seasoned professionals.

Security concerns may require that the daily routine and/or programs be cancelled at a moment's notice. Sometimes the reason cannot be explained, especially to outsiders. Other times, when tension builds inside the facility, inmates are locked in their cells long enough to cool down. Other times, inmates are "locked down" while staff conduct a search. While frustrating for the staff members, and especially to volunteers who may have traveled long distances at significant expense to donate their services, it is important to remember that this is simply a part of working inside a prison or jail.

Security concerns also require that everything be conducted in the open. New employees are frequently shocked at the lack of privacy afforded to them and to inmates. Almost all office doors have windows, and inmates frequently use open showers and toilets. Inmates are less likely to harm others or act improperly when their actions are open for anyone to see.

Screening Prospective Workers

Because of the security risks involved, before they are hired, prospective workers are screened to ensure their suitability for work in correctional settings. Workers may be required to complete lengthy written applications. They may be fingerprinted and photographed. Their criminal histories will be checked and previous employment verified. All the information obtained is kept confidential and may be used only to decide if the application should be approved. Bullies need not apply. Correctional facilities are looking for dedicated people whose goal is to become a team worker within the chain of command—to help each facility meet its goals.

A person's labor is of no value unless it helps the system. Unfortunately, people sometimes exaggerate their qualifications. Prospective workers should expect to provide copies of their credentials (e.g., state licenses, diplomas, or certificates). When approved, new workers are usually issued an identification card that allows them entrance into the correctional facilities. Being a correctional worker is a privilege. Breaking the rules can end that privilege.

Being a convicted criminal does not automatically exclude one from being a correctional worker. Although some specific jobs may be closed to those with criminal records, prospective employees who have criminal records should ask the personnel officer to explain prison or jail regulations. Some prison systems realize that a model of successful reentry into the free world provides valuable experience that can help inmates.

Prison officials learn from their mistakes. Over the years, thousands of people, including workers, have been caught bringing contraband into prison. This could be something as serious as illegal drugs or as minor as a type of jewelry that is not allowed in that facility. For this reason, everyone entering a prison or jail is subject to being searched. Many prisons search people at random. Although being searched can be embarrassing, accept it gracefully. It is necessary to make working inside the prison as safe as possible.

Becoming Part of the System

People who work inside prisons and jails are hired to provide specific services. Since each job is important, all members of the staff must learn to work together as a team. Support staff members must not interfere with the custodial responsibilities of administrators and security staff. Activities must be scheduled in strict accordance with existing institutional routines, rules, and regulations. Security staff members should cooperate with the support staff and not disturb programs unless absolutely necessary. Inmates are seldom helped in an environment where there is a power struggle between security and support personnel. Prisons and jails do not need employees who create additional problems.

New workers should show the entire staff that they are concerned about the staff's needs. Prisons may be rather depressing places to work. Many people make the mistake of thinking only about their own job and what they can do for inmates. In doing so, they begin copying the inmate's contempt for officers and other staff. This does not help the inmate, staff, or others working within the system. New employees and volunteers who become part of the team and realize that their job is to help staff perform their mission will find themselves earning the respect of both inmates and staff.

In *The Effective Correctional Officer*, Corrothers (1992) says: "There is no field of endeavor more exciting and challenging than criminal justice and no component with more opportunities to 'make a difference' than in corrections." The days of the ball and chain are gone. The essence of modern correctional effort requires everyone to work together as a team.

Today's correctional facilities are more than just a place to house inmates. Today's goals include helping inmates correct the patterns that keep getting them into trouble. Any worker who is not part of the solution is part of the problem.

Understanding the Criminal Personality

Teaching inmates the aspects of the criminal personality can be an effective way to help them change. It can help them see themselves as they really are. This is the first step in achieving any change.

Knowledge Prevents Disaster

Working inside a prison or jail without understanding the criminal personality invites disaster. Correctional staff workers cannot help inmates change until they understand the individuals with whom they are dealing. Even then, only some inmates will change.

As you read this chapter, please remember that inmates are individuals. Although many have common features, their individual differences should be taken into consideration before any labels are applied.

Treating each inmate with the dignity that he or she deserves can be an important first step in teaching inmates how to respect the feelings of others.

Research Helps Us Understand Inmates

Much of what is known about the criminal personality comes from the work of Samuel Yochelson and Stanton Samenow. Their research and published works identified more than fifty thinking errors criminal offenders display. Their research has become a foundation of many successful prison and jail programs (Yochelson and Samenow 1976, 1977, 1986; Samenow 1984). Prison psychologists Prem Gupta, Gad Czudner, and Ruth Mueller have duplicated many of Yochelson and Samenow's findings (Gupta 1984; Gupta and Mueller 1984; Czudner et al. 1984). This chapter presents a summary of the work by these pioneer prison professionals.

Research usually does not describe specific individuals. Instead, it provides descriptions of the average person in the group that was observed. Accordingly, the majority of criminals can be expected to display most of the characteristics discussed in this chapter. Likewise, some will exhibit all of these attributes, and others may not display any of them at all.

Having these traits does not make one a criminal. Becoming a criminal is a personal choice. Criminals are people who are thinking about, planning, or doing criminal acts. Teaching inmates the aspects of the criminal personality can be an effective way to help them change. It can help them see themselves as they really are. This is the first step in achieving any change.

The Criminal Mask

Masks are useful defense mechanisms. They allow people to continue working even when they feel their entire world is falling apart. Everyone wears them occasionally. However, most people know when to put their masks on and when to take them off. Although their private lives may remain private, "normal" people have nothing to hide. Since their actions match their perception of themselves, others are allowed to see who they really are.

Criminals are different. They *do* have things to hide. Thus, they wear a mask all the time. Like chameleons, they quickly change masks to be able to match their demeanor or behavior with their perception of the environment. For example, an inmate may show remorse or guilt while talking with a staff member or the parole board but may brag about his conquests to a group of inmates. One mask makes the inmate appear full of religious zeal, another allows this same inmate to "curse like a sailor" in a different setting. Many inmates learn to wear masks of responsibility, loyalty, and trust. Since most do not want to serve their entire sentence, they need these masks to convince people that they have truly changed. Criminals change their masks to suit different audiences.

There is a problem with masks. Nobody knows what the person wearing the mask is really like. Unfortunately, the average criminal feels too vulnerable to reveal his or her true self.

A Narcissistic Outlook on Life

Research shows that narcissism, or self-centeredness, is the central theme of criminals' psychological makeup. They view life, friendships, and even love with the thought of what they can get out of it. They are always asking, "What's in it for me?" Giving of themselves to help others is a foreign idea.

Self-centered people confuse need, desire, and control in a relationship with love. Some feel that narcissistic people are incapable of love. Gupta and associates suggest that criminals love themselves so much there is no room to love anyone else.

The American Psychiatric Association's *Diagnostic and Statistical Manual of Mental Disorders, Fourth Edition* (1994) defines a person with a narcissistic personality disorder as one who has at least five of the following qualities: (1) has grandiose feelings of self-importance and wants to be recognized as superior without earning the appropriate achievements to back this claim, (2) is preoccupied with self-fulfilling fantasies, (3) believes he or she is "special" and has unique problems understandable only by high status or other "special" people, (4) requires constant attention and admiration, (5) feels overentitled, (6) is exploitive, (7) lacks empathy, (8) is preoccupied with feelings of envy, and (9) shows arrogant, haughty attitudes or behaviors. Research shows that the average criminal displays all nine of these characteristics.

Criminals' self-centered nature prevents them from showing consideration for others. Altruism, generosity, gratitude, honesty, integrity, modesty, and tact are uncharacteristic of their way of thinking. They usually do not get along well with others.

Narcissistic people frequently strut around like the only rooster in a hen house. Their words and actions say, "I'm number one! I can do anything I want. Say anything I want.

Anytime I want. Anywhere I want. To anyone I want! And there is nothing anyone can do about it. Period!!"

A Need for Power and Control

The average criminal is motivated by a need to have power and to control the situation. According to Samenow (1984), criminals consider others their pawns. People are of value only if they bend to the criminal's will. The criminal attempts to accomplish this by force, intimidation, or manipulation.

Prison psychologist Czudner (1985) says that criminals often blame their activity on alcohol, drugs, the company they keep, lack of love or too much love when growing up, poor economic conditions, unemployment, or a host of other excuses. The truth is that criminals do their crimes because they want to do them and enjoy them while they are committing them. However, criminals do not enjoy getting caught.

They crave the excitement that comes from having the power to make victims yield to their demands. Creating and living by their own laws makes them feel even more in control. For example, drug dealers enjoy the power of having people beg for their product. Thieves and robbers enjoy forcing people to give them their property. Sex offenders enjoy the self-proclaimed power to pick any man, woman, or child and force their victim to have sex with them. Murderers enjoy the power of having control over life itself.

Many criminals act on impulse. They enjoy the power of not having to control their urges. To the average criminal, "might makes right." Being in control becomes more important than the relationship itself. Even sex is motivated by power and control. It becomes a way to boost the criminal's ego.

This need for power and control does not stop when criminals go to jail or prison. The typical criminal tries to dominate every situation and will resort to any tactic to get his or her own way. The most obvious form of this is when criminals simply refuse to obey institutional rules.

Manipulation is a form of overpowering. An inmate may appear to be genuinely remorseful, but in the same breath, the inmate will ask the staff member to break a "small" rule to help him or her. If this does not work, inmates may try angry outbursts or constant pleading until they get their way. Other inmates resort to tears.

Another way of controlling is refusing to listen to another point of view. Compromise is out of the question. Frequently, inmates will pretend to be helpless so someone else will do their assignments.

Criminals have the power to change. Changing means they have to give up their self-proclaimed power and live by society's rules. Many inmates are unwilling to pay that price.

A Lifestyle of Lying

Most people lie occasionally. To some, telling a "white lie" may be preferable to telling a friend that his or her cooking is terrible. To a criminal, lying is a way of life. It feeds the criminal's basic patterns. Yochelson and Samenow (1976, 1977, 1986) claim that to choose to be in crime requires one to lie for self-preservation.

Some people feel that lying can become such a habit that it becomes compulsive. Yochelson and Samenow disagree. Their studies indicate that criminals can readily distinguish between the truth and a lie. They are ready to tell either depending on which will do them the most good. Criminals can become such good actors that they can lie while looking you straight in the eye. Many of them tell the lies for so long that they actually start believing them.

Even when criminals tell the truth, it is frequently some form of a con game. Criminals tell enough truths to gain the listener's trust, then they start lying. They sometimes tell half-truths, thus convincing themselves that they are, indeed, honest. They forget that distortions or anything less than the whole truth is a lie.

Lying is a way to get out of trouble. Many criminals will enlist others to help them lie. Some years ago, a man broke into a warehouse. During the investigation the police found several of his fingerprints. In court, he and his family swore that they were out of the state when the crime happened and that he had never been near that warehouse.

One sex offender set up a camcorder to record his crime. The video was found. He still insists that he is not the one on the tape.

Deep inside, criminals think of themselves as good people. To prove this, they will point out how good they are to their family. For example, some incest perpetrators will insist that they were a good parent to their victims.

Criminals' lies are often their downfall. Living one's life telling half-truths requires a good memory. It requires remembering which half of the truth was told to whom. Fortunately for the authorities, most criminals are not as good at remembering as they are at lying.

Antisocial Behavior and Lack of Responsibility

Antisocial behavior is how the criminal personality is expressed. Criminals' deeds fail to conform to society's norms. They repeatedly do deeds that are grounds for arrest, including cheating, stealing, vandalizing, engaging in physical cruelty, harassing others, or having an illegal occupation. Antisocial people tend to be irritable and aggressive. They also are known to repeatedly get into fights and to commit assaults, including spouse and child beating.

Antisocial individuals have little regard for the personal safety of others. Reckless driving, driving under the influence, and repeated abuse of alcohol and other drugs are common. Sexual promiscuity is the norm. They have few genuine friends.

Early in life, antisocial people begin feeling that they are "different" from everyone else. As a result, many decide to go it alone. This isolation from others prevents them from learning that many others share their concerns.

Responsibility is understanding one's obligations. This includes one's duty to family and society as a whole. Most criminals like the idea of having children. It boosts their ego. However, some men feel no obligation to provide for their family's support.

As a group, antisocial people appear unable or unwilling to keep a steady job. They do not keep appointments, and they have difficulty keeping promises. In classroom settings, they do not follow rules, and they fail to do homework assignments.

Criminals' lack of responsibility keeps them from succeeding in life. Many can sit for hours and talk about the big dreams they hope to achieve when released. Yet, few ever follow through by doing the tasks necessary to achieve those dreams. Instead, they are always looking for a shortcut to fame and financial freedom.

Most people understand that breaking the law brings with it an expectation of punishment. Criminals will avoid responsibility by trying to make it appear that someone, or something else, *made* them do their crime. Many blame their victim or society.

Others blame drugs. Some wear the tattoo "born to lose." This allows them to make fate responsible for their actions.

Low Frustration Tolerance

"I want what I want when I want it" could be the guiding principle for most criminals. Like a two-year-old child, when they want something, they want it now. When criminals' wishes are blocked or delayed, they immediately become angry. This aspect of the criminal mentality prevents them from completing tasks that require sustained effort. When the "going gets tough," he or she gets going—away from the job or responsibility.

According to Samenow (1984), many criminals are remarkably talented. Prisons are full of talented artists who have had little formal training. It is (usually) a joy to listen to inmates sing or play musical instruments they have learned to play by ear. Some are excellent craftspersons. The quality of the leatherwork, furniture, and children's handmade toys can be excellent.

One of the sad aspects of working in a jail or prison is seeing raw talent going to waste. It is even sadder to see inmates take little interest in training and apprenticeship programs. These take perseverance, but most inmates want instant success.

Some inmates lose interest because they are not disciplined enough to take advantage of the opportunity. Others are so afraid of failure that they give up without trying. The criminal is likely to be turned off by the process of learning. Many feel that it is foolish to learn to do hard work when it is easier for them to gain instant gratification (and money) through crime.

This is frustrating to prison and jail workers. In many cases, staff members will see inmates take the first steps toward positive change, then suddenly quit. Many inmates will blame the instructor, counselor, or other staff members for making it difficult for them to participate. The truth is, in most cases, the criminal simply has not acquired the skills to handle the frustration that comes from trying to complete an assignment.

Distorted Ideas About Love

Criminals can be charming, talented, and bright. They can display affection and appreciation. Usually, this is a mask. When criminals talk about love, they are usually thinking about what love can do for them. Doing something to make the love reciprocal is a new idea to most criminals. As a group, criminals frequently use and manipulate people they love for their own objectives.

For example, most inmates claim to love their mothers. After all, she is the one who has continued to believe in him or her. She has probably been the source of bail money, and she may have paid the attorney. She always accepts the collect phone calls. She is also likely to be rearing the inmate's children. And, in spite of how poorly the criminal may have treated her, she has never given up hope. This is the inmate's kind of love. Inmates have a hard time understanding that receiving love is not the same as loving someone.

Mature love is giving a part of yourself that is the best you have to offer, asking nothing in return but that the gift be accepted. It is never given for selfish reasons, never for personal gain. It is the accepting and exchanging of gifts of love that causes the relationship to grow.

Inmates, especially men, have a difficult time showing love. Prisons are filled with narcissistic people who only look out for "number one." Many are afraid because they equate love with sex. This fear prevents them from changing their distorted ideas about love. The average inmate feels that displaying kindness and respect are signs of weakness. As a result, caring people become targets for manipulation.

Violence and Anger

Although many inmates wear a mask of calm and control, it usually covers a raging anger that lies just below the surface and frequently erupts into fights and angry words. This anger may appear to be out of control, but it is not. For example, most "spontaneous" fights stop instantly if the warden appears. Instead, its use depends on the criminal's perception of the situation with which he or she is dealing.

Violence and anger also are useful to invoke fear or to intimidate others. Other times they are used to cover fear or to create a tough appearance. Violence and anger can even emerge as depression designed to evoke feelings of pity. Regardless of the form in which these traits are displayed, they are an attempt to force others to give the criminals their own way.

Lack of Remorse and Guilt

Criminals often confuse guilt with being caught. In a study of a randomly selected group of Alabama inmates, the inmates were asked several questions. One of the questions asked, "Does a person violate the law, even if he is never charged?" Over 58 percent circled the incorrect answer: "he is *in fact* innocent of that crime until proven guilty" (Bayse 1989). Some inmates hold firmly to the belief that they do not *actually* become guilty until a court says they are guilty. Others have insisted that they would *in fact* become innocent if the conviction were overturned by an appeals court. Many inmates find it hard to believe that, convicted or not, criminals become guilty the moment they commit a crime.

Guilt can be a healthy emotion. In *Emotions, Can You Trust Them?*, Dobson (1980) says that appropriate guilt is a message from your conscience that says: "You should be ashamed for what you have done." Guilt should be a guide for moral action. However, to enjoy the fruits of their crimes, criminals must suppress these guilty feelings. Instead, feelings of appropriate guilt are replaced with the uneasy feeling that comes with the fear of being caught.

Over the years, inmates have created innovative ways to convince themselves of their innocence. According to Harris (1991), the criminal's rationalizations usually fall into distinctive categories. Many will simply deny their guilt in spite of overwhelming evidence. One inmate who was photographed by the bank's security camera while cashing a forged, stolen check still denied his guilt. His fingerprints were found on the check, and the forged signature matched his handwriting. He claimed that he was in another state and that someone who looked like him stole his driver's license and used it for identification.

Others will blame the victim. One inmate, serving a life sentence for killing a state trooper, claimed that if the trooper had not pulled his gun when he reached for his, he would not have *had* to kill the trooper. Sex offenders often claim that the way the victim was (un)dressed *caused* the crime.

Others find fault with the system. This reminds me of a cartoon showing an inmate talking to a correctional officer. "I want to see the warden," the inmate says. To which the correctional officer replies, "Let me guess, you are totally innocent of the made-up charges that put you here. The judge was crooked, and the police officers and witnesses lied on the witness stand.

And, besides that, your attorney did not represent you properly." "Hey," the inmate exclaims, "I see that you've already heard about my case!"

Others feel that they were entitled to commit their crimes because of some past injustice. For example, many claim that perceived improper action by the police entitles mobs to riot, loot, and terrorize neighborhoods. Many inmates attempt to justify their actions with words like, "I did what anyone would do in a situation like that." Some years ago in Richmond, Virginia, a man was charged with killing his wife. He had found her in bed with another man. In court, the judge asked the defendant why he killed her instead of her lover. He replied, "She was so unfaithful that if I killed him, I would have had to kill another one next week."

Still others will claim that society's ills, their home environment, or their own insanity is the reason for their crime. Saying that alcohol or other drugs "caused" them to do their crime is becoming an increasingly popular defense.

These excuses are designed to make it look like the crime was not the criminal's fault, but the criminal was really a victim. Because of this, many criminals do not see any reason to feel remorseful for their actions.

Lack of Empathy

Criminals, as a group, do not have the ability to empathize: to put themselves in someone else's shoes. This is a skill that is necessary for anyone who desires close interpersonal relationships. Close friends are those who can share each other's pain and joy.

Yochelson and Samenow's (1976, 1977, 1986) research shows that criminals have little concern about the effect of crime on their victims. Frequently, they will deny any harm was done. Common to their thinking are words like: "He wasn't really hurt when I stabbed him. He only spent a few hours in the hospital, and he recovered in a couple of weeks." Or, "What are they so mad about? The insurance company took care of the damages. It didn't cost them anything."

Child molesters frequently say, "I didn't really hurt her (or him). All I did was touch." Rapists frequently use a similar statement, "She didn't really get hurt. After all, I didn't cut her or anything." Many inmates have no concept of the lasting emotional harm that is done when a person is a victim of a crime.

Inmates as a whole do not understand how their actions have hurt their families. For example, research (Bayse 1982) has shown that 49 percent of inmates agreed that "anytime you do something in your home that proves you to be untrustworthy, it gives the family a chance to practice forgiveness and makes the family stronger."

Although it is difficult, inmates can be taught to respect the feelings of others. It is only then that rehabilitation can begin.

Labels Can Be Dangerous

The danger in generalizing about inmates is that some people will assume that all inmates fit this stereotype. This is not the case: inmates are individuals. Although many have common features, all people who work in prisons and jails should treat each individual inmate with the dignity that he or she deserves.

Inmates:
Our Reason
for Working

There is never enough time, unless you're serving it.

—Malcom Forbes

Crime: The Great Equalizer

Prisons and jails hold people of all socioeconomic groups, ages, races, and genders. Everyone from former presidential aides to skid-row bums has lived there. Inside, it is not unusual to see a former doctor sleeping next to a former construction worker. Former ministers share cells with former drug dealers, former college professors with the illiterate. Yet, their uniforms tend to make them all look the same.

A majority of inmates feel their crime was caused by unmanageable, powerful, external forces. Most have sad stories to tell. To offer only sympathy reinforces the inmates' idea that they are the victim of these external forces.

Inmates have decisions to make, lives to restore. Most genuinely do not want to come back to prison or jail. Only a few have the skills to make that dream come true. Security staff, support staff, and volunteers must work together to help inmates discover, understand, explore, try, and take responsibility for their options. It takes the coordinated efforts of the entire team to help inmates realize that they have the power to change. Only then can inmates begin feeling like capable human beings who have the ability to survive in the "free world."

Imprisonment Changes People

Inmates live in an atmosphere of deprivation where each day seems like the one before. Once inside the walls, inmates lose most of their independence and control over their lives. They are stripped of legitimate power and most of their possessions. Their status is that of a social outcast. Separation from families and other meaningful aspects of life leaves many feeling abandoned and desolate.

There are many natural responses to living in this type of environment. Frustration, fear, anger, depression, and feelings of hopelessness are common. Inmates, like all of us, try to adapt to their surroundings. Some of the ways they adapt are healthy. Included in these are seeking counseling, participating in programs, and maintaining contact with families and friends. Others, such as conforming to the inmate code and manipulating people, are not.

Inmates, submerged in their feelings of alienation from society, create their own social standing. Unfortunately, this is based on their accomplishments in crime. At one end are the heroes—the murderers, especially cop killers. At the opposite end are the sex offenders—child molesters are considered the lowest of the low.

Inmates live with other inmates. Because of this, many inmates become "prisonized" or "institutionalized." This occurs when inmates begin accepting the attitudes, norms, values, and behavior patterns of more hardened criminals. Criminal skills are honed in prisons. Prisonized inmates usually return after they are released. Research shows that one effective preventive measure is for inmates to have continual contact with people from the "free world." This is one of the reasons that having volunteers in correctional facilities is so important. It helps inmates focus on becoming part of their community once again.

This is also one of the reasons that visits are so important. More than fifty years of research have shown the strong positive relationship between the strength of the family's social bonds and the ex-offender's successful reentry (Homer 1979). Homer also presented evidence that only 2 percent of those with three or more regular visitors had to be sent back to prison while on parole. On the other hand, those with no visitors were six times more likely to reenter prison during their first year of parole than those with three or more visitors.

This is one area where staff members can make a difference. Helping volunteers become part of the team and, within the limits of security, helping to make family visits pleasant experiences can reduce the prisonization process. This, in turn, can help to make the facility a safer place to work.

Life Behind Bars

Prisons are not nice places to live. A common complaint among inmates is the feeling that no one can be trusted. Their every move is watched by correctional officers. Because of this, they live with the feeling we have when there is a police car in our rearview mirror. Many inmates will act friendly just so they can find out things about other inmates. Then, if they think it will be beneficial to them, they will gladly tell prison officials the other inmate's secrets. As a result, many inmates are afraid to make friends.

Inmates always fear being set up for a fall. Many inmates are released on parole. As a means of control, inmates will frequently do things that will hurt other inmates' chances for an early release. These could include planting contraband, filing false charges, or trying to start fights with an inmate to cause that person to be "locked down" on the day of his or her hearing.

Inmates have little or no privacy. Windows or bars allow constant observation. In many places, inmates are not even trusted to go to the toilet or shower in private. They are watched because prison officials know that body cavities offer a popular way to smuggle drugs in or transport them throughout the correctional system. The correctional officer watching may be of either sex. Equal employment opportunity laws require this.

Inmates are subject to being searched at any time. In some cases, these searches require inmates to remove their clothing or allow their body cavities to be examined. This requirement is necessary to keep weapons or other forms of contraband out of the prison. The threat is real. One Alabama prison has a copy of an x-ray mounted on the wall showing a small automatic pistol an inmate had hidden in his rectum.

In *Breaking into Prison*, Buckley (1974) tells of an inmate who had a visitor continually bring in an abundant supply of dental floss. The visitor grew tired of this, but felt sorry for the inmate because the prison did not supply dental floss. One day when the visitor came, the inmate was gone. The inmate had used the dental floss to fashion a ladder and escape. Inmates are always looking for ways to beat the system and for ways to get staff members to help them do it.

Incoming mail is opened and checked for contraband. Schedules are set. Meals are served at prescribed times. Even the serving trays and utensils are chosen with security in mind. Griping about the food is a favorite pastime. Part of the loss of power includes the inability to choose when, where, and what one eats.

Inmates quickly discover that their sexuality does not stop when they enter prison or jail. There are few, if any, legitimate outlets for sex. This causes a lot of pain. Many fights are caused by the homosexual advances of other inmates. The lack of privacy can make any sexual activity, even masturbation, an embarrassing public event.

Many inmates blame the system and feel there is little they can do to control their lives. Some regain power by "giving in" and learn to placate those in authority. Others rebel. Conflict is inevitable. Some use the time to learn from their mistakes. These are the ones who can be helped.

Inmates in Jails

The Department of Justice (June 1992) reports that during the year ending June 29, 1990, there were nearly 20 million admissions and releases in the nation's jails. Its August 1993 report showed that the average daily population for 1992 increased 4.9 percent over the previous year to a record 441,889. On June 30, 1993, locally operated jails and correctional facilities held a record 444,584 people. The Department of Justice (August 1992) statistics indicate that this figure has increased 77 percent during the past six years. Drug violations were responsible for 40 percent of this increase.

According to the Department of Justice (August 1993), 91 percent of the jail inmates were male and 9 percent were female; 40 percent were white and 44 percent were black. Hispanics accounted for 15 percent of the jail population.

On the average, jail inmates spend at least fifteen hours per day in their cells. Only half had work assignments. The most common work assignments included: janitorial, maintenance, office, and food service duties (Department of Justice, March 1992).

Prison Populations

The Department of Justice (June 1994) statistics show that at the end of 1993 the population in state and federal prisons reached an all-time high of 948,881. Of these, 65,225 were admitted during the latest year. About 80 percent of these inmates had either been in prison, in jail, or on probation before beginning their sentence (Greenfeld 1992). Prison populations have more than doubled in the past ten years, due in large part to drug and alcohol use. Two-thirds of inmates serving time for a violent offense were under the influence of alcohol or other drugs when they did their crime (Department of Justice 1991).

The Criminal Justice Institute (1994) reported that the average age for 1993 admissions was 30.6 years old. On January 1, 1994, the racial mixture in prisons was 48.9 percent white, 37.8 percent black, 8.2 percent Hispanic, and 2.9 percent Native American. Other races accounted for the remainder.

In *Prisons and Prisoners in the United States*, Greenfeld (1992) says that the inmate's average prison sentence was 6.1 years, with approximately 24 percent receiving sentences of 15 years or more. On the average, inmates were released after serving 34 percent of their sentences. At least 123,000 of the 386,228 inmates who were released in 1989 were expected to return within three years (Criminal Justice Institute 1990).

Male Inmates

A study (Bayse 1989) of Alabama medium security male inmates revealed that their years of education ranged from 2 to 19, with an average of 11.1 years. Only 19 percent were legally married. However, 48 percent were presently involved in a long-term relationship with a significant other. The remainder were single. A large majority of the inmates (46 percent) were still attached to their legal wives or significant others. Only 18.5 percent divorced between the time of their arrest and present imprisonment. Although 32 percent of the inmates were child-less, the remaining 68 percent had produced an average of three children each.

Inmates frequently enter prison with their family relationships in distress and rapidly deteriorating. The inmates in the Alabama study were no exception. Slightly more than half were less than happy with their present family relationships. In that study, the more self-centered the inmate, the more disengaged he felt from his family.

Although this research applies only to Alabama inmates, the figures are consistent with current research and with inmate groups in other states. For example, twenty-three inmates who participated in a life seminar in Oklahoma listed a total of thirty-one marriages and thirty-four "common law relationships." The nineteen inmates who had children listed sixty-four children and twenty-five grandchildren. Most were less than happy with their family relationships. Unfortunately, most of them were also unaware of the concepts of normal family functioning and basic parenting skills.

Male prisons are "macho" places where the strong survive by acting or being tough. Few male inmates have any real plans about what they will do once they are released, except for some vague plans about the great job they will find. Unless some intervention changes their thinking, most will return to the same "hard living" lifestyle that put them in prison in the first place.

Female Inmates

Female inmates have always been in the minority. Since 1990, jail populations have averaged approximately 10 percent women. Prisons held 6 percent women. Female inmates face many issues that are similar to those faced by men. These include: the lack of marketable job skills, the need to eliminate criminal thinking patterns, and the need to learn relationship and/or parenting skills. Both sexes need to learn that they have the power to break the chains that bind them to their past improper actions and establish a new and productive life once released.

Women also face many issues that are different than those faced by men. For example, Department of Justice (March 1992) statistics found that about 44 percent of female inmates reported that they had been either physically or sexually assaulted at some point in their lives. Observation by prison professionals suggests that the actual figures are much higher. Women are more likely to have been emotionally close to the victims of their violent crimes. In general, female inmates have used more drugs and have used them more frequently than male inmates.

When a man goes to prison, his family usually maintains supportive contact. This is not so with women. Riggs and van Baalen (1992) found in a small study that male inmates received twice the number of visits as did female inmates. For women, prison can be an especially lonely place.

Many women enter prison as a single parent. Others give birth in prison. Less than 25 percent of the fathers are willing to assume custody. Many mothers lose their children to foster care. Female inmates, much more than their male counterparts, grieve over the loss of their children and regularly voice their concern about their welfare.

As a group, women are not afraid to show their emotions and express their feelings. They are more likely to self-disclose in groups. However, most also know how to use their behavior and/or emotions to manipulate others. For example, crying can have an emotional effect on staff members. When this happens, correctional workers must make a quick assessment and decision. In some cases, it is important to comfort and deal with the issue causing the pain. On the other hand, if the crying is an attempt to control, it is important to get on with the agenda of the meeting.

Prison officials in Alabama, Wyoming, Maryland, and the Bureau of Prisons have indicated that unlike male inmates, female inmates have a need to be touched. Although touching is more tolerated in prisons for women, it presents a delicate problem. Sound correctional practices require a professional distance be maintained between inmates and staff members, including volunteers. Some women are seductive and will use an "innocent" flirt to start the process. Men, in particular, need to be aware of this. People who work with female inmates should understand their institution's policy about touching inmates before they begin their duties. They should discuss this with their supervisors.

Throughout the ages, women have established their identity and found fulfillment by nurturing others, providing for their children, and building secure relationships. As a group, they thrive on intimacy and being connected to special people in their lives. To replace what they had to leave behind, female inmates frequently create pseudofamilies inside prison walls. As on the outside, these "families" usually have problems. Issues of dominance, jealousy, and physical, sexual, or emotional abuse are common. Many need help as they balance their need for intimacy and relationships with the limits of their own morality. Staff members and volunteers alike must be careful not to allow themselves to become manipulated into assuming a leadership role in one of these "families."

Inmates Are "Cultural" People

Crime knows no cultural barriers. Unfortunately, racial prejudice still exists within prison walls, just as it does on the outside. Discrimination has no place in correctional service.

Lambert (1991) notes that culture is a learned experience. It is how one generation shares its attitudes, beliefs, values, and behavior patterns with the next generation. One's culture could include languages, foods, traditions, customs, and learning styles.

By respecting an inmate's cultural heritage, you show respect to that individual; therefore, staff members need to be aware of cultural differences. For example, Cesarez and Madrid-Bustos (1991) say that showing respect to Hispanic men may require reprimanding them one-on-one and away from their peers. Many Native Americans feel that looking someone in the eye shows disrespect.

Many inmates come from impoverished, dysfunctional, minority families. As a result, deep resentments stemming from years of discrimination are common. Because of this, many have learned to distrust people of different races. Overcoming this requires that staff members demonstrate a basic respect for each inmate and his or her culture. However, many inmates use cultural differences as an excuse for breaking the rules and/or their criminal activity. Over the years, many staff members have been manipulated into falling in this trap.

Showing respect to inmates includes understanding the background that helped place them inside the walls. However, understanding their values does not require you to agree with them.

Inmates Live by the Inmate Code

Part of becoming prisonized is learning to live by the "inmate code." Life inside prison is a constant power struggle between the criminal element and the rules of the system. This code allows inmates to create and live by their own rules without fear of punishment. Inmates enforce this code with a vengeance. Violations are met with sanctions ranging from ostracism to physical violence, or death, especially in maximum security prisons.

As explained in the training materials used by the Kansas Department of Corrections, there are six chief tenets of the inmate social code:

1. **Be loyal.** There seems to be an unwritten rule throughout prisons that says inmates must be loyal to each other. This includes maintaining a "code of silence" about criminal activities done by other inmates. Inmates are expected to lie, if necessary, to protect other inmates who they know have violated the rules. This loyalty is demanded regardless of the personal cost to the individual inmate. Inmates are never to take a problem to prison staff. Doing so would be considered a breach of loyalty.

2. **Be cool.** Inmates are always to be in control. They are to refrain from quarrels or arguments with fellow inmates. They are to remain cool regardless of how much pressure they receive from correctional staff. Their slogan seems to be: "Just do your time and do not make waves."

3. **Be straight (with your fellow inmates).** Do not take advantage of another inmate. Do not lie. Do not break your word. Do not steal. Pay your debts. Inmates should share with one another by exchanging goods for gifts or favors. Unfortunately, many inmates break this rule, causing friction among inmates. Being straight with a staff member is telling enough half-truths to get off or doing what is necessary to get one's way.

4. **Be tough.** Do not weaken, do not whine, and do not cry "guilty." The inmate should be able to "take it" without quivering. Although the inmate code discourages inmates from starting a fight, running from a fight that someone else starts is considered disgraceful.

5. **Be sharp.** Do not be a sucker. Correctional officers are to be treated with suspicion and distrust. Whenever there is a conflict between an officer and an inmate, always assume that the correctional officer is wrong.

6. **Be right.** This is a combination of the other five. An inmate is "right" when he or she is loyal to fellow inmates. Inmates can depend on him or her. The right inmate

never interferes with another inmate's schemes to break prison rules. He or she does not back down if someone picks a fight. "Right" inmates know their rights and use them to get their way. They can take whatever the prison system dishes out and never flinch.

Inmates Are Narcissistic

As explained earlier, narcissism or self-centeredness is the average inmates' most prominent feature. They look out for "number one." Narcissistic people concentrate on getting their own needs met. They expect others to give them what they desire without complaint. In fact, putting the needs and feelings of others ahead of their own is considered by inmates to be a sign of weakness.

Narcissistic people live by their own rules. Since these types of people see kindness as weakness, any display of concern is likely to be met with an attempt to control. Tardiness, constant trips to the toilet, failure to do assignments, or dominating group discussions are the norm. So is simply getting up and leaving.

A consequence of being self-centered is the inability to see how one's actions affect others. As a result, they cannot understand the way people feel about what they have done. Yet, these same inmates will protest loudly if another narcissistic inmate insists on having his or her own way.

Inmates Have an External Locus of Control

Social scientist Heider (1958) defined locus of control as a personality variable referring to the feelings of control that individuals *perceive* they have over their lives. Emotionally healthy people have an internal locus of control. They realize their lives are controlled by their ability and/or the amount of effort they expend to complete tasks. People with an internal locus of control feel they have the power to choose their own destiny.

Researchers have known for years that people who feel in control of their lives are usually happier and more successful than those who do not feel in control. People with a strong internal locus of control realize they have the ability to rise above their present situation. This enables them to build better lives for themselves. They learn from their mistakes. What they lack in ability, they make up by putting out the extra effort to get the job done. People like this fully understand the meaning of the adage: "You'll never know how much you can do until you've bitten off more than you can chew."

Unhealthy personalities, including criminals, have an external locus of control. They feel that their lives are controlled by luck, the difficulty of the task, or power of others. Many inmates grew up in homes where they were physically, sexually, or emotionally abused. An external locus of control is easily formed in abusive homes where the child's life is literally controlled by the anger or sobriety of the parent.

Most inmates believe that external forces control their lives. Because of this, they feel powerless to choose their own behavior and/or chart their own destiny. They blame their crimes on external forces. Many honestly believe that someone or something other than themselves caused them to do their crime.

Many Inmates Are Religious People

Religion can be very important to inmates. For some, it becomes an innovative way to meet their own needs. Con-artists have done this for years. In *Breaking into Prison*, Buckley (1974) describes a lawsuit filed by a group of inmates complaining about the lack of religious freedom inside the prison. The suit asked the court to require the prison to recognize their "Church of the New Song" and to require the prison to furnish the materials for its liturgy—steak and wine for all of their followers.

And with the passage of the Religious Freedom Restoration Act (RFRA), prison systems are starting to see inmate lawsuits asking for even more outrageous "religious freedoms."

Not all inmates are like that. Lonely cells and cold steel bars have a way of breaking the human spirit. Faith in God provides the promise of forgiveness, healing, restoration, and a new abundant life. Out of their desperation, many inmates reach out for that promise. For that reason, chaplains and religious volunteers find correctional facilities a field "white unto harvest."

Many men and women experience true religious conversions inside prisons and jails. Frequently, religious workers find that changes started in a jail will bear fruit by the time an inmate gets to prison. To fill their time, many inmates spend countless hours doing in-depth Bible studies. Some religious leaders feel that a nationwide, large-scale spiritual awakening may result from these studies. A study funded by Prison Fellowship Ministries found that inmates who participate in religious instruction while incarcerated have lower recidivism rates (Gartner et al. 1990).

Some changes are real and some are not. Inmates usually want staff members and volunteers to like them. As a result, many inmates will make repeated religious commitments simply to please the volunteers. One chaplain told of asking volunteers to provide the total number of inmates who made religious commitments during their services. At the end of one year, 2,100 inmates in that prison had made *first time* professions of faith in God. The prison only held 700 inmates.

Religious volunteers are frequently surprised to discover that prison officials do not share their excitement. Volunteers only get to see the enthusiasm displayed by inmates during services. Do not burst their bubble. As a correctional employee, you will see the results of "jailhouse religion." While true religion is a way of life, many narcissistic inmates want the forgiveness and acceptance that religion promises without having to follow the strict moral guidelines that are part of its teaching. It is not unusual for inmates to make a religious commitment and then ask, "Well, I've been forgiven, when do I get to leave?"

Correctional workers quickly learn not to take inmates' religious commitments at face value. Instead, they wait and see if the inmates' lives show positive change. You can help volunteers become part of the team by encouraging them to do the same. Religious freedom does not stop at the prison doors. Inside the walls are people of all religions. Followers of every faith are convinced that they have found the "One True God." Arguing rarely convinces anyone to change. It solidifies positions. In this case, it may be best to agree to disagree. Within the limits of security, staff members should ensure that all inmates of all faiths be given an opportunity to practice their religious freedom.

Many religious workers focus their attention on messages designed to convert inmates to their faith. This may be an appropriate message for a transient population such as a jail. The men and women in prison are long-time residents. They desire the same type of messages they would hear in their churches or synagogues back home. They want to know how to apply spiritual principles to their everyday lives.

Inmates Can Change

Correctional workers will frequently hear inmates say: "I just can't do it. It is just too difficult." This sentiment, which can be

intensified by the words of uncaring staff members, has pre-
vented many inmates from becoming useful and productive
members of society. Both security and support staff members
can demonstrate by their actions and attitudes their faith in an
inmate's ability to change. Inmates must be led to realize that
the word "can't" usually means "won't." Inmates must be helped
to realize the potential in their own abilities. Understanding how
much their lives would change if they made an effort would
empower them with the ability to make that change.

Effective Ways to Work with Inmates

Teamwork! Teamwork! Teamwork!

The adage "a house divided against itself cannot stand" is especially true inside of correctional facilities. An effective facility is an independently functioning community of correctional professionals working together to achieve the facility's goals. As Chase Riveland, secretary of the Washington State Department of Corrections, tells each new employee: "We all depend on each team member to do his or her part. Likewise, we should help each other achieve excellence so we may all succeed." Whether you work inside of a prison or jail, in the community, or at headquarters, you have an obligation to do your job well not only to help everyone else in your department but also for the citizens who pay your salary.

The Federal Bureau of Prisons' *Employee Handbook* says that the public is best served when inmates are kept busy in productive work, training, and educational pursuits. Like all people, inmates have spiritual, physical, emotional, and medical needs. Facilities need to be maintained and the work stations supervised. It takes dedicated people who can do each of these jobs well to keep the team operational.

Correctional facilities are training grounds where college students serve practicum and internship placements. With each of their programs, volunteers bring a message telling inmates that at least someone on the outside does care. Everyone wins when staff members encourage these "outside" people to cooperatively work together with staff. Some volunteers even make significant contributions. For example, the Alabama Department of Corrections used a graduate student to create, implement, and research its first family life psychoeducational programs.

Unfortunately, most inmates do not like living by someone else's rules. This is why the Illinois Department of Corrections tells its new employees that one of the most important roles in the correctional field is learning how to manage people. Keeping the facility safe while attempting to correct the dysfunctional attitudes, values, and behavior patterns of the inmate residents takes everyone's coordinated efforts.

Teamwork is learning to cooperate within a chain of command. Effective correctional work is giving 100 percent of who you are to fill your spot in that chain of command. It is understanding that no chain is stronger than its weakest link, being strong yourself, and working to make the other links stronger. *In correctional work you are either a part of the team or you are a part of the problem.*

Learn the Standard Operating Procedures

Every organization has rules and regulations. However, in corrections, knowing the standard operating procedures literally can save your life. Each regulation and policy was placed there for a reason, many times because of costly mistakes.

Inmates tend to be antisocial at times and prone to test the rules. As Massachusetts tells its new employees: "being conscious of their prison environment will enable you to fulfill your job function and help prevent you from falling prey to inmate influence. By being knowledgeable of all updated policies, procedures, and regulations, the threat of potential chaos can be reduced."

Inmates have a tendency to sue for all types of real or imagined injustices. Knowing and following correct procedure and the ethical standards of the profession (see the inside back cover) can do more than just help you keep your job—it can also "save your hide" in court.

Make Suggestions

Prison systems are always looking for ways to improve their operations. Thoughtful employees share their knowledge to make the workplace better. Check with your supervisor to see how the suggestions should be made. Some might be implemented immediately. Others, such as a suggestion for a new program, might require a detailed, written application and a multistep approval process. Suggestions or programs that appeal to a broad range of inmate or facility needs and interests are more likely to be approved than those that do not.

Having a great idea does not guarantee acceptance. Wise employees are willing to work with the system. Some make the mistake of trying to force their programs on prison officials. Prisons, like all places, can be difficult places to work if you are not part of the team.

Look the Part

All correctional staff members should dress appropriately for the positions they fill. If in a uniformed position, wear the uniform with the pride that it deserves. Not only does a sloppy uniform look unprofessional, some inmates consider it to be a sign of weakness. This can make you a target.

Regulations require that civilian clothing look different from the prisoner's uniforms. Business attire is preferred. Women should not wear heavy make-up or perfume. Tight, short, low-cut, or revealing clothing is not allowed. Do not wear clothing that could be considered seductive. For men, business attire usually means a shirt and tie, and no blue jeans. Earrings are prohibited in many places. Do not wear expensive jewelry or watches. Purses and briefcases should never be left unattended.

When in doubt, check it out. Avoid the embarrassment of being sent home or disciplined for wearing clothing that is considered inappropriate for that facility.

Stages of Effectiveness

As mentioned in the Missouri Department of Corrections' training materials, few if any of the people hired by prisons and jails enter as professionals. Becoming an effective correctional worker does not happen automatically. Effectiveness comes through training and experience.

Stage 1: "The Rookie"

Most new employees are full of enthusiasm and some apprehension about their new job in corrections. Some start by feeling sorry for the "poor lost sheep" and relate to them in a paternalistic or condescending manner. Others expect to be treated like royalty and demand that inmates obey their orders without questioning. Still others remain aloof or detached and treat inmates as if they were objects instead of people. This type of behavior is destructive to both inmates and the employee. Employees with these attitudes may do more harm than good.

Those who familiarize themselves with the department's expectations and listen to the more experienced employees without becoming cynical will have a better chance of getting through this stage.

Stage 2: "The Disillusioned"

During this stage, employees become angry with the system. The daily stress of working with antisocial personalities and within a chain of command wears their patience thin. Friendly conversations may be replaced with constant griping. Employees may begin openly questioning the administration's motives and the way programs are developed, and may become impatient with the many rules and regulations. Family problems, burnout, absenteeism, and alcohol and drug addiction may occur.

A shift usually occurs during this stage. The employees' focus on the things they dislike about their job makes them unaware of their own blind spots. As a result, these employees miss pathological or obvious criminal thinking patterns of the inmates that could cause problems. It is during these times that correctional workers are especially vulnerable to making critical errors in judgment that could cost them their jobs or even their lives.

Employees in this stage may not treat other staff members with respect. While this behavior may be popular with inmates, ultimately it is destructive to everyone involved.

For some, going through the stage of disillusionment is a ripple, for others a waterfall. The key to getting through this stage is to find someone you can trust (such as a mentor, employee assistance program, counselor, or minister) to help guide you through the turbulent waters. *Stressed Out: Strategies for Living and Working with Stress in Corrections* by Gary Cornelius provides some constructive suggestions to help you get through this stage (Cornelius 1994).

Stage 3: "The Professional"

During this stage, employees progress to a more balanced position by beginning to look at people and situations objectively. Issues will be faced in an open and honest manner. They begin learning the strengths and weaknesses of the personnel, programs, and the institution itself.

Correctional workers at this stage begin to see things realistically. They begin discovering how inmates, staff, security, and volunteers can complement one another. This allows the correctional process to become a collaborative effort. First impressions and overgeneralizations regarding staff and inmates are dropped. In their place comes an understanding of the adage: "You can't see eye to eye with others until you quit looking down on them."

Once correctional workers reach this stage, they can attend effectively to the needs of the facility and those they serve. They are useful because they have become a valuable part of the team.

How to be a Good Correctional Worker

Adults of all ages, most educational levels, and from all walks of life can become good correctional workers. Correctional systems need levelheaded people who are willing to share their experience or training with inmates and want to work cooperatively with other correctional employees. To be effective, correctional employees should:

Be Ethical

Every professional organization has ethical standards that guide its practice. The American Correctional Association's Code of Ethics is listed on the inside back cover. However, being ethical is more than simply following a set of rules; it is a way of life.

Ethical living means treating others with respect, no matter how they treat you. It is treating others the way you want to be treated. Ethical living means having nothing to hide. It is not caring who watches you or worrying about being seen in the "wrong place." Ethical living means doing what is right simply because it is the right thing to do.

Practice Good Communication Skills

Daniel Stieneke, Director of the North Carolina Department of Corrections Office of Staff Development and Training, says that effective communication is one of a correctional employee's most important tools.

Communication starts by listening. Everybody needs someone who will listen. Inmates and staff members are no exception. They experience joy, sorrow, happiness, and sadness just like everyone else. They need someone who cares about their thoughts and feelings. Listening to what inmates say makes their words valuable, enhancing their self-esteem. Listening to what other staff members say makes you part of the team.

Inmates will be cautious at first. Most have never had anyone who really listened to their needs. However, as inmates learn that you are trustworthy, they will begin opening up. Listen for themes in the conversation. What they repeat is probably what is bothering them.

Learn effective ways of speaking. It is possible to strictly enforce the rules, or even file a grievance against a supervisor, without resorting to profanity or other verbal attacks. This can literally save your life. In 1987 and 1991 there were three major disturbances inside federal prisons where large numbers of staff members were held hostage. The Federal Bureau of Prisons believes to a large extent that the reason these staff members were not brutalized was because Bureau staff had treated the inmates humanely in the years prior to the incidents.

Be Empathic Without Being Gullible

Empathy is showing others that you are willing to look at life from their perspective. It also involves communicating that understanding to them. Employees cannot be effective until they have an understanding of the pressures, needs, interests, capabilities, and limitations of the inmates from their point of view.

However, empathy does not require you to abandon your beliefs, values, or feelings. Nor does it mean that you must agree with the inmates' position. Instead, it is listening with the intent of understanding. It does not mean believing everything you hear. Some correctional employees overidentify and begin feeling *like* the inmates. This brings the employees down to the inmates' level and makes it harder for them to help.

Be Respectful

To be effective, correctional workers must simultaneously respect inmates as individuals, empathize with their pain, and believe in their capacity to change. There is no room for prejudice or feelings of superiority in a prison setting.

Will Rogers said: "I never met a man I didn't like." Most of us are less tolerant. The words "love the sinner but hate the sin" are easy to say. However, as Salter (1988) says, it is difficult to extend respect to people who frequently lie, con, deny, and minimize behavior that is harmful to others.

Sometimes, showing respect is being honest enough to withdraw. Occasionally, there may be inmates you simply cannot deal with because of their personality or crime. If this happens, talk it over with your supervisor. Admit that it is your problem and not the inmate's. Sometimes, it can turn the tide.

Let the relationship grow. Inmates, like others, require you to earn their respect and trust before they will open up. Respect is responding to the inmates' interests while still maintaining a professional relationship.

Do not pry. Let inmates decide when to reveal details about their crime, their past, or other concerns. Think about it: Do you enjoy people asking about your past just to satisfy their own curiosity?

Be Genuine

Being genuine is allowing people to see the real you. It involves expressing your true feelings with tact and consideration. It is being "straight" and talking without using words that have double meanings.

Genuine people also can take criticism without becoming defensive. They know themselves, including their strengths and weaknesses. When someone expresses a negative opinion about them, instead of being hateful, they will try to understand the other person's point of view. Genuine people are honest and will share their feelings if someone else's behavior makes them uncomfortable.

How can one become genuine? As Oklahoma's training material says, "Be your 'best' self, but be yourself." Inmates can usually spot a phony a mile away.

Be Patient

There are many sources of frustration in correctional facilities. Sometimes frustration can take root while waiting for the outside gates to open, especially if it is cold or raining. Prison schedules are subject to change at a moment's notice. Security takes first priority. A fight, a missing key, the suspicion that an inmate is missing, or another unexplained reason could cause the entire facility to be "locked down." When this happens, all inmates are returned to their cells. This could last for minutes, hours, or even days.

Things like this happen. Effective correctional workers allow time for the unexpected. Those who roll with the punches will earn the respect of inmates and staff members alike. It also saves a lot of ulcers.

Be Trustworthy

Effective correctional workers do not make promises unless they are prepared to carry them out. Inmates will test staff members, or call their bluff, just to see if they will indeed keep their word. Once you break their trust, you have lost them.

Being trustworthy includes telling inmates the limits of confidentiality. Not everything can be kept confidential. For example, not advising your supervisors about a planned escape could result in prosecution in some states. Learn the rules at your facility and be up front with inmates. Make it a policy to keep no secrets from your prison or jail supervisor. Make the inmates aware of this from the beginning; then, it is up to them to decide what they want to reveal to you.

Being trustworthy means being honest. There are times when being honest may mean that inmates or other staff members may have to face the consequences of their own improper actions. Good employees, and especially officers, live by the adage: "I'll die for you, but I won't lie for you!"

Being trustworthy is showing up on time and following the rules. It also means not allowing inmates to con you into helping them break the rules. Being trustworthy is creating a reputation for being dependable and faithful.

Be Confrontational

Confrontation is showing inmates the difference between their statements and their actions. This should be done in a normal tone of voice or even humorously. Hostile confrontation is seldom effective. In *Tough Customers: Counseling Unwilling Clients*, Ganley (1991) says that using confrontation appropriately helps inmates not to rely on minimizing, denying, and blaming their crime on external forces. Appropriate confrontation helps inmates see themselves as they really are. This, in turn, gives them reasons to change their ways.

Most inmates come from dysfunctional backgrounds. Stories they tell may tug on the heartstrings of any caring individual. This makes it easy to create an inappropriate relationship. Effective staff workers realize that a criminal's past may have been a contributing factor in his or her decision to break the law, but it did not *cause* it. Constructive confrontation helps inmates accept responsibility for their behavior.

When confronting inmates, Salter (1988) recommends responses such as "Give me a break! What do you mean one drink can't do any harm?" Or, "Do you really expect me to believe that you broke open the door just to get in out of the cold?" Or, "I can't promise that I will always agree with you, and I don't expect you to always agree with me. I can promise, however, to always be straight with you, and you will always hear it from me. Does that sound fair?" Inmates respect people who are honest and strong enough not to be manipulated.

Be Objective—Do Not Take Sides

Unless you are a supervisor, never interfere with a correctional officer in the performance of his or her duties. If you have questions or comments about the way a situation was handled, discuss them with your supervisor in private. Follow the chain of command if you wish to lodge a complaint. If an inmate tries to get you involved, respond in a way that shows you respect the rules. For example: "That is between you and the officer." Encourage inmates to use the facility's grievance procedure if they feel an officer or other staff member was wrong.

Sometimes inmates fear retaliation if they file a complaint against a correctional employee. On very rare occasions, it may be appropriate to help facilitate a meeting between an inmate and another staff member. Before you do, discuss the complaint with your supervisor. He or she can then decide how this complaint should be addressed and can contact the appropriate staff member. It is important for inmates to see that you will be supportive of them *and* that you will respect the chain of command.

Take Charge, but Never Lose Control

Sooner or later, you will be faced with a hostile inmate. The inmate may be angry with you or with the whole world. People in this frame of mind tend to forget that all individuals are still responsible for their own actions—even when angry.

The natural response to a verbal attack by an inmate is to become defensive or argumentative. Whenever this happens, you need to remind yourself that angry outbursts are frequently part of the "con game" and the criminal's need to manipulate and control. Above all, do not act shocked or respond in a hostile, sarcastic, or anxious manner. Always remember that if *anyone* can say or do anything to you that causes you to react in the way *they* desired, you may "win" the fight, but they have won the "war" because they won control.

Training material provided by the Illinois Department of Corrections suggests a better way. First, *quickly* size up the situation so that you can decide what action is appropriate for your own situation and the security of the facility. Sometimes this means listening until they run out of steam. Do not try to force the conversation. Listen to the inmates' grievances and let them vent their feelings. Find the information you need in a way that makes inmates respond to you without feeling put down.

Know your escape route. Sometimes, it is best to stand your ground; other times, it is best to retreat. Then, even if it means calling in reinforcements and/or using the appropriate force, control the behavior.

Make your decision and stand by it, even if it is a decision to delay making the final decision. Remember, giving an inmate a reason for your decision is not a sign of weakness. On the contrary, it is the best way to minimize future problems. Then, they will not have to go away guessing where you stand on the matter.

You can be as tough as nails and still treat people with respect. Confrontation, and even the use of force, can be handled without losing control and abusing the inmate. Truly "tough" people are those who are in control of their words and actions, even when they are angry.

Do Not Expect to be Thanked

Many inmates (and others) have never been taught how to say "thank you." Others find it embarrassing to show gratitude. As a result, correctional workers may never hear those special words. Frequently, staff members feel unappreciated and are tempted to quit. Once in a while we do get to see the fruit of our labor. This is what makes working inside a correctional facility worthwhile. Unfortunately, most of the time we must be satisfied

54

with the knowledge that our work is appreciated—usually in ways that we will never know.

Suggestions and Rules

Although some prison rules may seem pointless, they are necessary to maintain discipline. A lot of them have been created as the result of unfortunate incidents. For example, some prisons will not let women bring in lipstick or wear wigs inside men's prisons. This is to keep inmates from escaping by being disguised as women.

Correctional facilities from across the country sent helpful hints that contributed to this book. The following hints and regulations that apply to most facilities were developed from that information:

1. All staff are correctional professionals who contribute, either directly or indirectly, to forming and even "correcting" the behavior of those under our authority [Canada].

2. Fulfill the mission and be a good neighbor. Be part of the community. Participate in community service projects [Oklahoma].

3. Successful correctional careers are earned by attention to daily responsibilities and details. Develop the ability to communicate in a clear and concise manner. Make sure that you understand what the inmate is trying to express [North Carolina].

4. A major "career buster" in the field of corrections is staff's inability to maintain professional relationships with inmates, probationers, or the family members and friends of those individuals under our custody or supervision. No personal or business relationships are permitted between correctional employees and offenders; this is the rule [Florida].

5. Be honest and forthright with your peer group, your supervisors, and the inmates held in custody. Such behavior may not always be easy, expedient, or career enhancing at the moment. In most cases, it will prove to be a long-term winner [Texas].

6. We cannot treat all inmates alike because they are inmates any more than we treat any other group of people the same because they belong to a particular group [Oregon].

7. In making a decision, an employee should consider the inmate's behavior, the situation, the rules and regulations of the institution, and the inmate's rights. The rules and regulations of the institution are the most important factors. Experienced officers find that inmates, like most people, respond more favorably to mild or polite requests [Illinois].

8. You never know how "moral" you are until you are faced with the situation. The most dangerous perception you can have is "it can't happen to me." Request help before it's too late. Don't talk personal business with inmates [South Carolina].

9. Employees shall not disclose confidential information gained by reason of their public positions, nor shall employees use such information or their public positions for personal gain or benefit [Missouri].

10. Use appropriate language. Don't pick up inmate slang or vulgarity. Using language that isn't a part of your style can label you a phony [Arkansas].

11. Never assume that inmates will maintain confidentiality in their conversations; there is a high probability that the inmate(s) involved will relate information to other inmates, staff, or other parties [Federal Bureau of Prisons].

12. Keep everything in the open. Do not say or do anything with an inmate you would be embarrassed to share with your peers or supervisors [Kansas].

13. It is imperative that all employees be security conscious. To maintain a secure and safe environment in the institution, it takes the cooperation of all the employees [Pennsylvania].

14. Be aware that the possession of, the use of, or being under the influence of, alcohol or drugs while on institution grounds is prohibited [Ohio].

15. Don't discuss the criminal justice system, the courts, inconsistency in sentencing, or related topics. Although everyone is entitled to his or her opinion, what employees say can have serious repercussions in the dorms or with staff [Wyoming].

16. The ideal corrections employee is mellow. A mellow employee knows when to be soft and when to be hard and how to apply his/her knowledge appropriately. Becoming mellow requires discipline and experience [Michigan].

17. Inmates have no respect for staff members they can lower to their own level of behavior. They do maintain great respect for people who, regardless of pressure, can continue to provide a high level of dignity and professionalism—people they can emulate [Connecticut].

18. Proper physical fitness will improve your general health and prevent injuries. It could also be important in preparing you to respond in the event of an emergency [Washington State].

19. If you've committed a minor indiscretion, acknowledge it and take the consequences—blow the whistle on yourself. Don't let the inmate escalate the process onto more serious issues [Massachusetts].

Dealing with Self-centered Inmates

As explained earlier, narcissism is the most prominent feature in the average inmate's personality. Self-centered people live by their own rules. This can make it difficult to lead or control groups in correctional settings.

Kiser (1987) describes the problems he had with inmates in a college-level class he was teaching. Several students refused to answer the roll. One refused to give his real name. Others wandered in and out of the classroom at will. Some stood in the hall for a while and simply stared into the classroom. Another refused to wait his turn while exams were returned and tried to pressure the professor into giving him his exam back first.

This story is not unusual. Inmates will do this and more just to demonstrate who actually has the power in the group. This means that instructors must decide how much of this type of behavior will be tolerated and take control of the group. Mallinger (1991) tells of an inmate who loudly announced, "I feel lousy today, so nobody better mess with me." Equally loudly, Mallinger responded, "I feel like writing a misconduct report today, so nobody better mess with me." They parted amicably.

Rules must be explained and enforced with politeness, firmness, and consistency. This helps inmates learn that every action has consequences, some good and some bad. Through sensitive confrontation, inmates can be taught to demonstrate care and respect for others. Caring confrontation may also include asking or forcing unruly inmates to leave. Inmates often associate caring with weakness, so to be effective, instructors must display "loving toughness."

Dealing with Inmates' External Locus of Control

As discussed earlier, most inmates have an external locus of control. These inmates feel their lives are controlled by luck, the difficulty of the task, or powerful others. As a result, they feel grades or completion certificates are arbitrarily assigned by instructors.

The accompanying feeling of powerlessness can drain inmates' motivation to complete rehabilitation programs. Their attitude seems to be "It won't help, so why learn?" Others will do what is minimally required to get their completion certificates or simply sit in class and not try.

This can be changed by showing inmates that they do have the power to complete rehabilitation programs. This requires programs to be designed with structured tasks that can be completed step by step. Program effectiveness will be increased if inmates know in advance *exactly* what they must do to successfully complete the program. They must *perceive* that these goals are within their grasp.

For example, to successfully complete the *As Free As An Eagle* family life psychoeducational programs (Bayse 1989), inmates must meet three requirements: (1) they must be present and on time during all the group sessions, (2) they must turn in all homework assignments, and (3) they must score at least 70 percent on the final exam. They understand that the rules are suspended only if prison staff require a change or for an emergency. Breaks are given every hour so that going to the toilet or getting a drink of water is not considered an emergency. Inmates know that failure to comply with any of the requirements is actually a request not to be allowed to graduate. They also know that the instructor can be *trusted* to comply with their request.

There is a grace period of ten minutes (by the instructor's watch) at the beginning of each class. During that time, the material on the final exam is reviewed. Inmates are taught during the first session that the rules are supported by staff and designed to help them develop responsibility. It is emphasized that they will need this skill to get out of prison and stay out.

The first session begins with the question, "Who will determine if you will pass this course?" Invariably, the inmates will reply, "You." Four questions are then asked:

1. "Since the warden cleared your schedule, can you get here on time?"

2. "Can you turn in your homework?"

3. "Since the exam will be reviewed, can you study enough to make at least 70 percent?"

4. "Who will determine if you pass this course?"

The reply now becomes, "I will." After starting the program with these questions, the average grade on the final exam has risen approximately ten points.

Inmates need to be taught that their success or failure will be determined by how well they fulfill class requirements. Inmates who perceive that they have the ability to successfully complete the requirements of programs will be the most successful.

Beating Inmates at Their Own Games

Creating and strictly enforcing the rules emphasizes the link between behavior and its consequences. It also allows instructors, officers, and other staff members to model ways of being in control while submitting to the external control of prison regulations. This includes using the chain of command, requesting that conflicting appointments be changed, submitting to security requirements, and working with staff members.

Language can be altered to confront criminal thinking patterns by introducing the concept of "earning" punishments. For example, instead of "What did the correctional officer give you for disobeying the order?" ask "What did you *earn* when you decided to disobey the correctional officer's order?" Statements such as "the judge *gave* me ten years" can be rephrased to "You mean you *earned* ten years the moment you committed the crime." To help them with their future, ask: "Once you are released on parole, what will you *earn* if you violate the conditions?" This can be followed with, "Isn't that like screaming 'Warden, I demand that you let me back in prison'?"

Since most inmates do not have internal controls, external deterrents to crime must be stressed. These include fear of being caught, fear of injury, or fear of doing more time. Using internal deterrents such as "don't do crime so you won't have a guilty conscience" are probably ineffective. A better statement to use might be: "Don't do the crime if you can't do the time."

Even though correctional systems are controlling systems, effective staff members show inmates how they can still have some control over their own destinies. Learning to be dependable and faithful can begin inside the prison walls. Pointing out how the inmate feels when he or she is the victim of narcissistic behavior is a good way to teach respect for the feelings of others.

Overcoming Inmate Resistance

Sometimes the use of force is necessary to overcome inmate resistance. However, in the majority of cases, other methods might be more appropriate. In *Counseling the Involuntary and Resistant Client,* Harris and Watkins (1987) say that resistance is necessary to help people hang onto their identity. The most obvious forms include: open hostility, silence, strained politeness, defensiveness, avoidance, and silliness. People display these behaviors for personal gain. Sometimes it is to overpower and get their own way. In other cases, the resistance is a reluctance to make suggested changes. In either case, inmates must see a reason to change before they will drop their resistance. Some resistance is caused by the inmate's inability to tolerate frustration. Change takes time. Inmates want an instant fix. They want what they want when they want it.

The use of metaphor is an effective way to overcome resistance. This could include a story that challenges inmates' thinking patterns, a parable that teaches a value, a joke with an appropriate punch line, or images. The image of a bull in the china shop can help inmates overcome their use of anger as a means of resistance and/or control.

Frequently, inmates will say, "You can't help me because you don't live here. You just don't know what it is like!" This can be countered with, "You're right, I don't know what it is like to live here. However, I do know how to live in the free world. Would you rather teach me how to live in here or learn how to live in the free world?"

At other times, inmates who refuse to acknowledge their criminal act may be asked, "What would happen if you began to remember and found out that you actually were guilty?" This allows them to save face and not appear to be a liar if they "suddenly" begin to remember at a later date.

Sometimes, inmates will remain resistant no matter how hard you try. Change is scary for most people. For criminals, giving up lifelong patterns means restructuring their entire world. Most will not apply the energy required to do this. But correctional staff members should keep trying; they may be planting a seed that will bear fruit later.

Theory of Change

The cognitive moral theory for changing criminals, developed by Gupta and associates (Gupta 1988; Gupta and Mueller 1984) is based on the premise that people have as much capacity for doing good as for doing bad. Using this theory requires helping inmates through five stages. First, help inmates quit making excuses for their actions and accept responsibility for their own actions. Although alcohol, drugs, lack of love or too much love, and socioeconomic conditions are contributing factors, they do not cause people to commit crimes. Criminals commit crimes because they choose to and they enjoy it.

Second, help them to become aware of the unfairness of the crime's effect on others. Teach them to see how much their crime has cost them and how much it has hurt their families. Use the information found in Chapter 2 to teach them the aspects of the criminal personality and to help them see how self-centered they really are.

Inmates have reached stage three when they start experiencing appropriate feelings of self-disgust and true guilt for the harm they have done. Stage four is using those feelings to motivate the inmate to make a commitment to change. Stage five involves helping the inmate to develop a plan to build a new and productive life.

Using Education to Produce Change

Mace (1981) claims that several steps must be taken before people change in response to education. First, the information must be given and the material understood. People must select the pieces of that newly learned knowledge that might apply to their own lives and experiment with the new concepts. Then, as they make commitments to use the new knowledge as a basis for growth, change can occur.

Helping Inmates with Their Religious Beliefs

Staff members frequently will hear statements such as "I've turned my life over to God, and I know that He will keep me out once I'm released." This, of course, makes a "powerful other" responsible if the inmate fails.

Statements such as these can be countered with illustrations from the Bible. For example, Exod. 4 shows that God did not stop Moses from killing the Egyptian, nor, as 2 Sam. 11 says, was David stopped from having an affair with Bathsheba and having her husband killed. These examples and others can be used to convince inmates that God allows individuals to follow their own desires. He also allows them to earn the consequences of their own decisions.

Inmates need to understand that faith in God is not enough to create change. It takes a commitment to learn *and* follow the moral guidelines of their faith. Encourage them to seek the help of the chaplain or a religious volunteer to show them how to accomplish this task.

Helping Inmates to Heal Themselves

The following five concepts can help inmates end their criminal careers (Bayse 1991):

1. **Teach them how to love.** Show them that love is giving a part of yourself that is the best you have to offer, asking nothing in return except that the gifts be accepted. True gifts of love are never given for selfish reasons or personal gain. Rejecting gifts of love is rejecting the giver of the gift and not the gift itself. Accepting and exchanging gifts of love will cause relationships to grow. Since love is something that you do and not something that you feel, anyone can start the loving process. It takes a strong person to show true love.

2. **Teach them how to forgive**. Forgiveness is not forgetting; we do not have the ability to forget. Forgiveness is a decision to treat the person as if the incident never happened, while still holding them accountable for their actions. Being held accountable is to ensure that it does not happen again.

   Forgiving themselves requires that they admit their wrongs to the people involved and accept the consequences of their own behavior. They pay their debts to their family, their victims, and society by doing their time, changing their lifestyle, and making any needed restitution. Then, help them to accept the fact that they now have a clean slate. Show them how to stop punishing themselves and start living the rest of their lives as if their moral failures never happened. Inmates must understand that this is hard to do. It becomes especially hard when they face unforgiving people who constantly remind them of their failures.

3. **Give them the gift of self-esteem**. Self-esteem, and the feeling of completeness that follows, has four aspects: feeling loved, feeling accepted, feeling competent, and following ethical principles. Staff members can help inmates develop self-esteem by showing them how to develop these four aspects. Showing them respect and acceptance will fulfill the first two requirements. Helping them to develop areas of competence and teaching them how to practice ethical living will give them the ability to achieve the others.

4. **Teach them the keys to freedom.** It takes two keys to open the door to freedom. They are (1) respecting the rules of society and (2) taking responsibility for one's own actions. Teach inmates how to use these keys.

5. **Teach them to dream.** Everything we ever accomplish starts with a dream that says: "I wonder what it would be like to (fill in the blank) ." Help them to start dreaming about what it would be like to be a useful part of family life and society once released. Then, give them the tools to achieve that dream.

Healing Involves Pain

Pain is a very useful feeling. One of the worst things that can happen to someone is to lose the ability to feel pain. When this happens, they can be hurt and not know it. Over the years, many inmates have lost their ability to feel emotional pain. Because of this, many have never had to accept responsibility for their own actions. *Life Beyond Loss: A Workbook for Incarcerated Men* (Welo 1995) provides inmates an opportunity to work through their grief and losses.

As inmates begin to realize how much grief they have caused others, their personal pain can become almost unbearable. They earned that pain, and staff members should not attempt to take it away. Instead, acknowledge their pain, but let them feel it. Help them realize that this pain is the consequence of their own actions. It is part of what they earned the moment they committed the crime. It is not something that someone else did to them. Surgery hurts, but the healing it produces makes it worth the pain.

Effective pain relief requires forgiveness and living a new lifestyle that does not cause more pain. Remembering the pain of past mistakes is an effective motivating tool.

5

Avoiding
the Pitfalls

Many problems in correctional facilities could be solved if staff members would model the keys to freedom: respecting the rules of the system and taking responsibility for their own actions.

Exercising Poor Judgment and Being Conned

Over the years, many have begun working in correctional facilities with the hope of helping inmates and beginning promising careers. Some have left in shame. This chapter is designed to help employees recognize and avoid some of the common pitfalls correctional workers face. Sometimes all it takes is one slip to start a landslide that can bury your reputation, your career, and your freedom.

In one institution, an inmate used a friendship with an officer that began in childhood to first convince the employee to pass messages to and from the inmate's mother, then to bring in a winter coat. The coat contained drugs that were sewn into the lining.

Two officers lost their jobs after being convinced to place $1,500 into an outside "bank account" to purchase a nonexistent motorcycle from an inmate. In another case, a prisoner convinced three correctional employees to spearhead an investment scheme to raise money to recover the treasure from a sunken Spanish galleon. Stock certificates were printed in the prison print shop and sold to their friends. All that was recovered from their $50,000 investment was a lot of heartache and pain.

The June 2, 1992, issue of *The Montgomery Advertiser* carried a wire story about a criminal justice professor who was charged with helping two men break out of prison. He told police that he gave the inmates a cutting tool because he was in love with one of them.

Mallinger (1991) tells of a librarian who was conned by an inmate who shared her love of poetry. He convinced her that it would be no big deal for her to smuggle some poetry books from his girlfriend into the prison. Unknown to the librarian, the books had drugs hidden in the bindings. When caught, the inmate eagerly told officials who brought the books to him. The librarian lost her job and was banned from ever working in another prison in that state.

Another employee, considered exceptional by his peers, was later arrested after soliciting the help of an inmate to find someone to kill his wife. As this former employee said: "working inside the facility didn't prepare me for living here."

One officer enjoyed "shadow boxing" with inmates. After about six months of this, an inmate "slipped" during one of the mock sparring sessions and knocked out several of the officer's teeth. Charges against the inmate were dismissed because he "accidentally" hit the officer.

We all make mistakes, and correctional employees make enough to fill a book. Fortunately, most are not as serious as the ones reported here. However, having to correct blunders creates a lot of tension inside of facilities. Being part of the team can help prevent mistakes like these from happening.

Problem Areas

The confining nature of a correctional environment creates an uneasy truce between inmates and the prison staff. Sometimes employees tend to be overconfident and insensitive to the problems inherent in a correctional facility. Because of this, some employees do more harm than good.

Some create problems by becoming angry with the system. Effective employees understand that the need for security overrides any other need in a correctional facility. Still, some inmates protest loudly if searched. This makes officers look even harder because they know that the people who howl the loudest frequently have the most to hide. Helping inmates starts by modeling willing compliance with security requirements.

Many employees have an inflated view of the good they can accomplish. Many get excited when they see inmates make what appear to be changes. Others, who do not see the expected results, become discouraged quickly. These people have fallen into the "instant success" trap. Change occurs slowly. Workers who see "instantaneous" change are usually reaping the harvest of previous work done by other team workers. The ones who do not see any apparent changes may have planted seeds that will blossom later.

Many workers become angry when other staff members display negative attitudes. This sort of problem should be handled through the chain of command. If you are having problems with another staff member, make sure you are not the source. Others, anxious to be the "good guy," help inmates perpetuate the idea that some other staff members or the administration are the "bad guys." These attitudes are not the way to gain the cooperation of your colleagues.

Being gullible can cause big problems. Many inmates can tell the biggest lies with the straightest face. Take everything you hear with a grain of salt. Horror stories of assaults, strip searches, homosexuality, drugs, and abuses by officers abound. Some are true. Most are not. Inmates, like many people, thrive on rumors, allegations, and gossip. The stories are designed to win your sympathy.

You will see and hear many things in a correctional facility that you will not understand. When this happens, talk to your supervisor before forming an opinion. Know and use your chain of command.

Many problems in correctional facilities could be solved if staff members would model the keys to freedom: respecting the rules of the system and taking responsibility for their own actions.

How Employees Get Conned

The word "con" can be defined as smooth talk used to extract a violation of regulations. It works. Sometimes employees are tempted to say, "They don't follow the rules, so why should we?" If you ever find yourself becoming willing to bend a rule to help an inmate, you have just become a prime target for being conned. It is not the weak employees who usually fail. Instead, as South Carolina Department of Corrections officials say: "it is usually good employees who would have been appalled at the suggestion that they would someday be caught doing something that would get them fired."

Inmates have lots of time on their hands, and they are constantly watching for employees who they feel would be susceptible to manipulation. They listen to conversations and watch constantly to find a "duck" to target. Most likely candidates are employees who are discontented with the job, having marital or financial problems, under stress, or experiencing anything else the inmates perceive as a weakness. Then, just as they did on the streets, they use this information to play a deadly "game" designed to fulfill their desires for drugs, sex, goods, services, and most of all—power.

Some setups take advantage of spur of the moment opportunities. Others are elaborate schemes carefully orchestrated by several inmates working together until they get the employee to do something that would result in severe employee discipline. Michigan training materials reveal that inmates will work an average of nineteen months on a single employee to achieve this goal.

The setup usually begins with the inmate(s) working to gain the employee's confidence and trust. Allen and Bosta (1981) suggest that in many cases the initial breakdown of professionalism is for an employee to go on a first-name basis with an inmate. Bonds are created that may gradually go beyond the limits of professional ethics. Favors beyond what are authorized for everyone will be requested to test the limits of the relationship.

Then, the inmate may try to convince the employee to violate a small rule that might even be considered common courtesy in another occupation (e.g., Will you mail this for me? May I have a stick of gum or a cigarette?) or violate a rule in the presence of the employee to see what will happen. The inmate gains power if the correctional worker violates policy. Such a minor violation allows for the gradual increase of demands until a major breech of rules is demanded. In many cases, out of fear of the discovery of past "wrongs," the employee yields to the demands and earns the destruction of his or her career.

This does not have to happen to you. In a videotaped teleconference, South Carolina Department of Corrections officials warn their employees that a smart person will always have someone they can go to and say: "I've got a problem and need some help." This mentor should be one who demonstrates professionalism, training, compassion, and the ability to keep things confidential.

Prison and jail administrators have an investment in everyone. They know that it is best for all concerned to salvage every employee they can. If the infraction was unintentional, most will do everything in their power to get a "fallen" worker back on track. Everyone is vulnerable.

As the Wisconsin Department of Corrections says in its training materials: *"If you have done something inappropriate, tell your supervisor regardless of what happened. It is far better to be reprimanded than to become a criminal."*

Not All Inmates Are Con-artists

Do not automatically assume that because an inmate is nice, he or she has ulterior motives. Not all inmates are manipulative. Some genuinely desire nothing more than a close working relationship with someone who cares. Nonmanipulative inmates will not be offended if they are told, "I'm sorry, but that's against the rules," or "I'm not sure, let me check with my supervisor." One of the best ways to keep from being manipulated is to never do or say anything you would not want to be made public.

Games Inmates Play

The following are six scenes correctional workers commonly face, dramatized in the National Institute of Corrections' training video, *Volunteer and Contract Service Employees*. They are all variations of the inmate con game.

"Just a Touch"

A female English teacher and a male inmate are talking after class. After a period of small talk and flattery, the inmate expresses concern about newly developing homosexual urges. "It's been three years," he explains, "can I touch you just once to reassure myself that I'm still a man?"

Ethical standards require that staff members maintain a professional distance from inmates. This is the only way to remain objective and focused on their needs. Should you discover that a relationship is building between you and an inmate, or if an inmate "comes on" to you, report it to your supervisor. Doing so can protect you later if the inmate tries to use it against you.

Romantic attraction and sexual involvement between staff members and inmates is a major problem in prison systems. Many inmates see any sign of caring as a sexual signal. Some inmates desire the relationship for the power it produces. Correctional employees who enjoy the flattery forget that most affairs start with "innocent" flirtation. "Forbidden fruit" usually ruins the lives of those who try it.

"Save Me from the Demon"

An inmate asks the drug treatment counselor to help him with plans for his imminent release. Fearing relapse, the inmate begs the counselor to accept him as one of his clients and rent him the room that is available at his house. "Just give me your name and address, and my brother will bring you the money to hold the room."

This is a common theme: "You are the only one who can help me." This theme includes requests to call wives, family members, or judges on their behalf. Although this is flattering, correctional staff members must be careful to maintain a professional distance from inmates. Instead, help them learn how to use the resources available to help themselves. Externally focused inmates frequently turn on the correctional workers, blaming them if the proposed intervention does not work.

Correctional workers should be careful of the information they provide inmates. For example, employees should never give their home phone numbers or addresses to inmates. It is not unusual for inmates to harass, beg assistance, threaten, or even harm trusting staff workers. If employees feel they have a legitimate reason for doing follow-up work once the inmate is released, it should be cleared with their supervisor before being offered.

"Easy for You, Sister"

An instructor is talking to an inmate who has done well in previous classes. Now, the student has stopped trying. Instead of accepting the instructor's challenge to use her talents, the inmate explodes, "It's easy for you to say, sister! You got your fancy job, your fine college degree, and you're doing your civic duty working in this joint." With that the inmate angrily runs out of the classroom.

Even though it is painful to watch, good instructors allow students to reap the failure they earn if they stop doing the work. It is not unusual for 50 percent of the students in a correctional setting to simply quit. The average inmate has a low frustration tolerance. Even though they may have the ability, many do not have the staying power to complete assignments. When this happens, externally focused inmates frequently blame the instructor for their failure.

It is important for instructors to understand the inmate's personality and provide continual encouragement. Instructors might consider pairing students so that the academically strong can help the weak. It is not manipulation to offer tutoring to inmates who request it or to review the exam content in class. Even if all of this is done, some inmates will simply sit in class but not try, then become angry because the instructor will not "give" them their diploma.

It is very important for instructors in a correctional setting to show that they cannot be manipulated into bending the rules. To avoid burnout, correctional workers should focus on inmates who *do* change and allow the others to reap the consequences of their own actions.

"They're Out to Get Us"

Inmates tell a staff member that two correctional officers are beating inmates for "kicks"—with the captain's permission. They claim to be unable to mail a letter to their attorney because the prison censors their mail. The scene ends with an inmate saying, "All I'm asking you to do is mail one lousy letter."

This is a typical con game. The common goal is to get the staff member to break a rule that would benefit the inmate. Many inmates have become experts at telling stories that would touch anyone. Some employees become callous and simply refuse the requests.

However, there is a slight chance that the story could be true. Unfortunately, cases of brutality do occasionally happen in prison. As such, these charges cannot be ignored. In this case, since a captain was accused, the staff member could offer to check with his supervisor and arrange a meeting with the appropriate official. He or she would find out quickly if the inmates were serious. If not, the inmates would say things like, "They don't care about us, so why bother?"

Variations of the same con game are asking correctional workers to make phone calls or bring packages from their "families" into or out of the facility. Employees may protect themselves from being conned by saying, "Let me ask my supervisor to see if it will be all right to do what you have asked."

Being asked to write a letter of reference is not part of the con game. This is a request commonly made to an instructor. If you feel that this would be appropriate, clear it with your supervisor first. A copy of the letter of reference should also be placed in the inmate's file.

"Not on the List"

An inmate is present who is not on the approved attendance list. The inmate claims staff forgot to include his name.

This does happen sometimes. Inmates also are known to attend functions to get out of their assignments. Instructors would be within their rights to ask the inmate to leave. Another response might be, "Let me check with my supervisor and see if it would be all right for you to stay."

"The Fight"

Two inmates start a fight in the classroom. The instructor panics, tries to get an inmate to stop it, runs past the telephone, and out of the room. As soon as she leaves, an inmate steals some items from her purse, which she left on the desk. She returns and calls for help.

If an inmate gets hostile, you should talk calmly and avoid being argumentative. Signal a staff person. If alone, maneuver yourself into the vision or hearing range of a staff member. If you have a whistle, use it. Do not attempt to resolve the situation on your own. Get assistance from staff—correctional officers are trained to handle such situations.

Prisons and jails are harsh places. Many inmates have spent their entire lives forcing their will on others through physical violence. Occasionally, they become angry enough to attack correctional staff members. If this happens, use the system. Require that the inmate face the consequences of his or her behavior by filing the appropriate disciplinary or criminal charges.

What About Riots?

Prison riots do happen occasionally. When they do, they make headlines across the nation. However, as Maryland's training material says, "the chance of being taken hostage is probably as remote as the possibility of being struck down by lightning." If a riot should occur, staff members should follow the training guidelines of the facility and remember that the security staff have received extensive training to respond to this event. Most riots end in less than five hours—without injury.

Planning for the unexpected can prevent catastrophe. Washington's training materials provide several suggestions for employees who find themselves held captive:

1. Do not act foolishly; heroics can get you hurt.

2. Be cooperative and comply with the captor's demands.

3. Look for a place to take cover, such as under a desk, in case authorities or inmates attempt to storm your area.

4. Keep a low profile, and avoid the appearance of observing crimes committed by rioters.

5. Do not make threats or attempt to negotiate with captors.

6. Try to act natural and listen if the captors want to talk.

7. Be observant and write down your observations as soon as you are released.

8. Seek counseling when it is over. Some things in life are not meant to be handled alone.

Keeping Up with Your Paperwork

The person who first said "A job is never complete until the paperwork is done" must have worked in corrections. Accurate records are needed to successfully operate any facility. In corrections, as in many jobs, if the facts are not put on paper in a timely and proper fashion, they become useless.

Memories fade, but accurate, properly filed documents do not. This can become crucial when inmates file frivolous complaints or litigation. Accurate records can help you if questions arise about your pay, vacation, sick leave, or travel reimbursement.

As you schedule your day, remember that completing the paperwork before you leave is part of that day's work.

Never Stop Learning

You have (or will) receive the basic training necessary to do your job soon after you are hired. But this is not enough to effectively do your job. The field of corrections is rapidly changing. Court decisions, new laws, and more effective methods of training, rehabilitation, and security are always being tested.

Continuing your education will allow you to learn more efficient ways of doing your job and keep you from repeating the mistakes of others. Sometimes this means attending conventions and training seminars. Other times it means reading the many books and articles that are now available.

Organizations of Interest

The **American Correctional Association** (4380 Forbes Boulevard, Lanham, MD 20706) is a multidisciplinary organization consisting of correctional professionals, individuals, agencies, and organizations involved in the entire spectrum of correctional activities. Joining this organization can help you stay abreast of the ever-changing world of correctional service. Reasonably priced memberships are available to correctional workers. Benefits include a subscription to the magazine *Corrections Today* and discounts on the many books published by ACA. For information, call 800-ACA-JOIN.

The **American Jail Association** (1000 Day Road, Suite 100, Hagerstown, MD 21740) is a professional organization dedicated to the improvement of the nation's jails. It produces a magazine, books, and videotapes covering a wide variety of jail training topics. For information, call 301-790-3930.

The **International Association of Addiction and Offender Counselors** is part of the American Counseling Association (5999 Stevenson Avenue, Alexandria, VA 22304). Membership is limited to professionals in the counseling or human development fields. Membership benefits include professional journal subscriptions, the availability of professional liability insurance, and a monthly newsletter. For information, call 800-347-6647.

The **Family and Corrections Network** (P.O. Box 244, Palmyra, VA 22963) is a national, professional organization that works to reduce crime by strengthening family ties. It shares skills and resources with people who provide programs and services for the families of inmates.

The **National Institute of Corrections Information Center** (1860 Industrial Circle, Suite A, Longmont, CO 80503) has a library of information available for use. For information, call 303-682-0213.

Avoiding Burnout

Generally, correctional workers do not seek employment inside a prison or jail for the money; usually, it is because they care. There simply are not enough hours in the day to fill all of the needs of the people housed inside. One of the biggest causes of burnout is trying to accomplish or promising more than you can humanly deliver. It is important to enter a correctional facility with clear guidelines of what you can realistically expect to accomplish in the time allowed. Judging yourself on this criterion will allow you to feel a sense of accomplishment and can help keep you from burning out.

In *Stressed Out: Strategies for Living and Working with Stress in Corrections*, Cornelius explains that "stress, if not managed properly, can have a definite effect on how correctional officers feel physically and also on how they behave toward themselves and others." However, "the good thing is that there is something [they] can do to reverse burnout. They can learn to manage their stress. Realizing that change is necessary is an important first step" (Cornelius 1994).

Avoiding burnout requires that you maintain a balance of activities and interests outside of the facility. It takes attention to your own spiritual, emotional, and mental health. Sometimes this includes seeking professional help when the pressures become too great. Participate in the wellness activities available in your community or at your facility.

Working with inmates is not easy. Many times you will want to throw up your arms and quit. This frequently happens when you look at the large number of inmates who refuse to change instead of the small number who actually do change. Success in correctional rehabilitation is measured one inmate at a time. Each one who is rehabilitated and becomes a useful member of society is no longer a criminal. Who can put a price on one changed life? That is why we choose to become correctional workers.

Glossary of Prison Slang

Notes from the field

In the early 1970s, I was called to a Virginia maximum security prison to investigate an attempted murder of one inmate by another. Right out of the academy, I was a "gung-ho" rookie trooper on his first case inside the prison. The primary suspect was an inmate serving life without parole for committing several murders. This big, burly, rough-talking man was the self-appointed "godfather" of the prison yard.

During questioning, the inmate became belligerent and threatened me. To show that I wasn't afraid, I looked him straight in the eye and said, "Listen, punk!" The inmate wanted to kill me and probably would have if the other correctional officers had not forcibly carried the inmate back to his cell—screaming threats all the way. I did not find out until later why I had almost caused a riot.

This glossary is included so that you will not make the same types of mistakes, including using slang. Do not expect to be treated like a professional if you do not sound like one. My second mistake was not knowing that inmates frequently assign different meanings to words than we do. For example, the word "inmate" means something entirely different than "convict."

This glossary was compiled from lists provided by inmates and prison systems from across the country. These definitions are not absolute—prison slang changes frequently.

—Daniel J. Bayse

Baby raper: Child molester

Blood: Inmate of the same race

Boss: (1) Supervisor, (2) term used in the southern United States for a correctional officer

Bounce: Try something (e.g., Bounce it off the staff and see if they'll go along with it.)

Box breaker: An inmate who steals from another inmate's locker

Brass: Prison or jail supervisors

Bug juice: (1) Artificially flavored, sweetened noncarbonated drink, (2) medicine

Bust your heart: A threat to kill

Buzzard: Someone who waits for a person to be raped by someone else before attempting to get sex from the victim

Candyman: Child molester

Case: A court charge (e.g., I was doing okay until I caught this case.)

Cludge: Gang up on someone and beat him or her

Coke: (1) any form of soft drink, (2) slang for cocaine

Convict: (1) Technically, an inmate, (2) slang for a hardened criminal, one who demonstrates little evidence of abandoning his/her criminal thinking patterns, and who lives by the inmate code

Cop a plea: Plea bargain, admit to a lesser charge

Cop talk: How inmates dismiss anything that suggests that they should live by the rules of society (e.g., That's just cop talk.)

Do-rag: Bandanna that shows gang affiliation

Doing a pound: A five-year sentence

Dope: (1) Drugs (e.g., You got any dope?), (2) information (e.g., Did you get the dope you needed to file your appeal?)

Drop a dime (quarter): (1) Inform on someone, being a snitch (e.g., He'll drop a dime in a heartbeat.), (2) make a phone call

Duck: a sucker, a mark: someone who is too soft or too hard, weak, gullible, stupid, or just asking to be taken advantage of

Duck head: Crazy person

EOS: End of sentence

Easy prey: A gullible person

Fall: Deliberately accepting the fault for something someone else did (e.g., I took a fall for my friend.)

Fall partner: Partner in crime

Free world: Life on the outside, anything other than prison

Fresh meat: A new inmate arriving at the prison, especially a young first offender

Gunning one down: Masturbating to a female correctional officer

Gunslinger: Masturbator

Hack: Correctional officer (see Screw)

Hit: (1) A dose of drugs, (2) to play on, ask for (e.g., I hit on him for some cigarettes.)

Homeboy, homie, honcho: Inmate from your hometown

Hooch juice: Homemade prison booze or smuggled-in liquor

Hot-rail: (1) Term used by inmates to inform fellow inmates that a correctional officer is coming, (2) a lookout who watches for security

Hustle: (1) being taken advantage of (e.g., See if you can hustle the volunteers out of their cigarettes.), (2) the way you make money out of the hobby-crafts

Ink slinger: Tattoo artist

Inmate: (1) Technically, someone who has been convicted of a crime and is housed in a correctional facility, (2) slang for a temporary resident of the facility; inmates show signs of rehabilitation and/or a desire to learn how to abandon their criminal thinking patterns and learn from their mistakes (see Convict)

Inmate code: See nothing, say nothing, know nothing

Instant biker: Someone who has a Harley Davidson tattoo, but knows nothing about motorcycles

Jailhouse Jesus: Claims to be a Christian but doesn't act like one

Joint: (1) Jail, prison, (2) marijuana cigarette

Jones: A habit you cannot break (e.g., I've got a jones for drugs and cigarettes.)

Jonesing: Coming down off a high and having no more drugs to create another high

Jumping the fence: (1) an escape, (2) leaving the convict role and becoming an inmate

Kick the bo-bo: Idle, meaningless talk

Kite: (1) Unauthorized or illegal letter, (2) a note (e.g., If you want to see the classification officer, send up a kite.)

Lever: Something that can be used against you

Lockdown: All inmates are confined to their cells; no inmate movement

Monkey on my back: A strong craving for alcohol or other drugs

Mule: Employee or volunteer who brings in contraband for inmates

Mule skinner: Homosexual male

On the streets: Outside of prison

Package: Nickname for contraband (e.g., Did you bring my package?)

Patsy: One who allows himself or herself to be used by others

Pearl handle: Brand-name, commercially prepared filtered cigarettes

Police: Anyone in authority, especially correctional officers

Pull his coat: Warn an inmate

Punk: A male who is willing to take the "female" or passive role in homosexual activity; being called a punk (or any other word symbolizing this) is considered *highly* offensive and has started many fights in prison systems (see Sissy or Queen)

Queen: A male who is willing to take the passive role in homosexual activity

Rap: (1) Talk, (2) conviction of a crime (e.g., took the rap)

Rap partner: Someone to talk with

Reefer: Marijuana

Screws: Correctional officers

Send you home to your mother: A death threat

Shakedown: Search an area in the facility without warning

Shank: Homemade knife or spear-like weapon

Shark: Inmate who loans to others for personal gain

Sissy: Homosexual male (see Punk)

Slick legging: Going through the motions of intercourse without removing clothing

Snitch: Tattletale

Snowman: Drug dealer—this may refer to someone who is willing to bring drugs into the prison or jail for inmates

Snuff out: To kill

Square: A cigarette

Stand-up dude: Dependable person

Stash: Inmate's personal storage of excessive amounts of any item, including drugs, cigarettes, soap, and toothpaste (e.g., How many cigarettes have you got in your stash?)

Store: (1) Prison commissary where personal items may be purchased, (2) the amount of money the inmate has in his or her personal account, (3) an illegal private enterprise where one inmate sells contraband goods to others at inflated prices

Stretch: Prison time served (e.g., She had a ten-year stretch.)

Sugar: (1) Homosexual, (2) someone special

Take it to the box: Jury trial

Ticket: Being written up for a violation of prison rules

Tight: Having a close personal relationship (e.g., That inmate and volunteer are tight.)

Tree jumper: (1) A rapist, (2) child molester

Wasted: (1) Killed, (2) dead drunk (e.g., I got wasted before I did my crime.)

Weed: Marijuana

Zip: Zero, nothing (e.g., He didn't get zip.)

Bibliography

*Items in **boldfaced type** may be ordered from the American Correctional Association. 1-800-825-BOOK.*

Alabama Criminal Code Annotated §§ 13A-8-5 (1978 as amended). "Theft of property in the third degree."

Allen, B. and D. Bosta. 1981. *Games Criminals Play: How You Can Profit by Knowing Them.* Susanville, Calif.: Rae John Publishers.

American Correctional Association. 1989. *Correctional Officer Resource Guide.* Laurel, Md.: American Correctional Association.

——. 1992. *The Effective Correctional Officer.* Laurel, Md.: American Correctional Association.

American Psychiatric Association. 1994. *Diagnostic and Statistical Manual of Mental Disorders.* 4th edition. Washington, D.C.: American Psychiatric Association.

Andrews, W. 1970. *Old-Time Punishments.* Detroit, Mich.: Singing Tree Press.

Arkansas Department of Correction. n.d. *Volunteer Manual.* Pine Bluff, Ark.: Arkansas Department of Correction.

Barnes, H. E. 1972. *The Story of Punishment: A Record of Man's Inhumanity to Man.* 2d edition. Montclair, N.J.: Patterson Smith.

Bayse, D. J. 1989. "A Study of the Effect of Family Life Education on Prisoners' Narcissism, Locus of Control, and View of Ideal Family Functioning." Master's thesis, Auburn University, Alabama.

——. 1991. *As Free as an Eagle: The Inmate's Family Survival Guide.* Laurel, Md.: American Correctional Association.

——. 1993. *Helping Hands: A Manual for Volunteers in Prisons and Jails.* Laurel, Md.: American Correctional Association.

Bayse, D. J., S. M. Allgood, and P. H. Van Wyk. "Family life education: An effective tool for prisoner rehabilitation." *Family Relations* 40 (1991):254-57.

Bayse, D. J., S. M. Allgood, and P. C. Van Wyk. "Locus of control, narcissism, and family life education in correctional rehabilitation." *The Journal of Offender Rehabilitation* 17 (3/4): 47-64 (1992).

Buckley, M. 1974. *Breaking into Prison: A Citizen's Guide to Volunteer Action.* Boston, Mass.: Beacon Press.

Cesarez, G., and J. Madrid-Bustos. "Taking a multicultural world view in today's corrections facilities." *Corrections Today* 53 (7): 68-71 (1991).

Connecticut Department of Correction. n.d. *Prison Environment Inmate Con Games.* Hartford, Conn.: Connecticut Department of Correction Center for Training and Staff Development.

Cornelius, G. F. 1994. *Stressed Out: Strategies for Living and Working with Stress in Corrections.* Laurel, Md.: American Correctional Association.

Correctional Service Canada. n.d. *Protecting Information and Assets in a Correctional Environment: Staff Handbook.* Ottawa, Ontario: Custody and Control Division, Correctional Service Canada.

Criminal Justice Institute. 1990. *The Corrections Yearbook: Instant Answers to Key Questions in Corrections.* Salem, N.Y.: Criminal Justice Institute.

———. 1994. *The Corrections Yearbook: Instant Answers to Key Questions in Corrections.* Salem, N.Y.: Criminal Justice Institute.

Czudner, G. "Changing the criminal: A theoretical proposal for change." *Federal Probation* 49 (3): 64-66 (1985).

Day, S. J. "Religious service program volunteer pre-service guide." State of Maryland Division of Correction, Religion Service Program, Baltimore, Md., 1992. Unpublished manuscript.

Dobson, J. 1980. *Emotions: Can You Trust Them?* New York: Bantam Books.

Earle, A. M. 1896. *Curious Punishment of Bygone Days.* Chicago, Ill.: Herbert S. Stone & Co.

Federal Bureau of Prisons. n.d. *Employee Handbook.* Washington, D.C.: U.S. Department of Justice.

Ganley, A. L. 1991. "Perpetrators of domestic violence: An overview of counseling the court-mandated client." In *Tough Customers: Counseling Unwilling Clients,* ed. G. A. Harris. Laurel, Md.: American Correctional Association.

Gartner, J., et al. "Final report on year one: Prison Fellowship research project." Prison Fellowship Ministries, Washington, D.C., 1990. Unpublished research project internal report prepared by the Institute for Religious Research, Loyola College in Maryland.

Glicken, V. K. and M. D. Glicken. "The utilization of locus of control theory in treatment." *The Indian Journal of Social Work* 2 (1982): 173-85.

Greenfeld, L. A. 1992. *Prisons and Prisoners in the United States.* Washington, D.C.: U.S. Department of Justice.

Griffith, J. "Evidence of unidimensionality of locus of control in women prisoners: Implications for prisoner rehabilitation." *Journal of Offender Counseling, Services and Rehabilitation* 9 (1/2): 57-69 (1984).

Gupta, P. K. 1988. *Case Management in Corrections.* Guelph, Ontario: Guelph Correctional Centre.

Gupta, P. K. and R. Mueller. "The correction of criminal thinking and behavior through the cognitive-moral approach." *Correctional Options* 4 (1984): 27-29.

Harris, G. A., ed. 1991. *Tough Customers: Counseling Unwilling Clients.* Laurel, Md.: American Correctional Association.

Harris, G. A. and D. Watkins. 1987. *Counseling the Involuntary and Resistant Client.* Laurel, Md.: American Correctional Association.

Heider, F. 1958. *The Psychology of Interpersonal Relations.* New York: John Wiley and Sons.

Hibbert, C. 1978. *The Roots of Evil: A Social History of Crime and Punishment.* Westport, Conn.: Greenwood Press.

Homer, E. L. "Inmate-family ties: Desirable but difficult." *Federal Probation* 43 (1): 47-52 (1979).

Illinois Department of Corrections. 1991. *Supervision of Inmates, Module 16.* Springfield, Ill.: Illinois Department of Corrections.

Jankowski, L. W. 1992. *Correctional Population in the United States, 1990.* Washington, D.C.: U.S. Department of Justice.

Kelly, Gregory P. 1991. *Anatomy of a Setup: Inservice Training Manual.* Lansing, Mich.: Michigan Department of Corrections.

Kiser, G. C. "Disciplinary problems among inmate college students." *Federal Probation* 51 (3): 42-48 (1987).

Lambert, J. "Training staff to take a new approach to today's diverse inmate population." *Corrections Today* 53 (7): 168-71 (1991).

MacDonald, A. P., Jr. "Internal-external locus of control: Parental antecedents." *Journal of Consulting and Clinical Psychology* 37 (1): 141-47 (1971).

Mace, D. "The long, long train from information-giving to behavioral change." *Family Relations* 30: 599-606 (1981).

Mallinger, S. "Games inmates play." *Corrections Today* 53 (7): 188-92 (1991).

Maryland Department of Public Safety and Correctional Services. 1989. *Operation Manual for Maryland Division of Correction Volunteers.* Baltimore, Md.: Maryland Division of Correction.

Missouri Department of Corrections. n.d. *Employee Handbook.* Jefferson City, Mo.: Missouri Department of Corrections.

——. n.d. *Basic Training Materials.* Jefferson City, Mo.: Missouri Department of Corrections.

National Institute of Corrections. 1984a. *Volunteer and Contract Service Employees.* Boulder, Colo.: National Institute of Corrections. Videotape.

——. 1984b. *Volunteer and Contract Service Employee Training Instructor's Manual.* Boulder, Colo.: National Institute of Corrections.

New York Department of Correctional Services. n.d. *Guidelines for Volunteer Services.* Albany, N.Y.: New York Department of Correctional Services.

Oklahoma Department of Corrections. n.d. *Leader's Handbook.* Oklahoma City, Ok.: Oklahoma Department of Corrections.

Oregon Department of Corrections. 1993. *Staff Training Section: Employee/Offender Relationships.* Salem, Ore.: Oregon Department of Corrections.

Parker, Bill and Joseph Wheeler, III. 1992. *Module 007: Working in a Correctional Environment.* Raleigh, N.C.: North Carolina Department of Corrections.

Pennsylvania Department of Corrections. 1989. *Security Orientation.* Elizabethtown, Penn.: Pennsylvania Department of Corrections.

"Professor Says He Helped in Escape of Lover Inmate," *The Montgomery Advertiser*, June 2, 1992, 3a.

Riggs, C. and S. van Baalen. 1992. "The pastoral needs of women in prison." In *Female Offenders: Meeting Needs of a Neglected Population.* Laurel, Md.: American Correctional Association.

Romig, C. A. and C. Gruenke. "The use of metaphor to overcome inmate resistance to mental health counseling." *Journal of Counseling and Development* 69 (5): 414-18 (1991).

Rotter, J. B. "Some problems and misconceptions related to the construct of internal versus external control of reinforcement." *Journal of Consulting and Clinical Psychology* 43 (1975): 56-67.

Salter, A. C. 1988. *Treating Child Sex Offenders and Victims: A Practical Guide.* Newbury Park, Calif.: Sage.

Samenow, S. E. 1984. *Inside the Criminal Mind.* New York: Times Books.

Schmalleger, F. 1986. *A History of Corrections: Emerging Ideologies and Practices.* Bristol, Ind.: Wyndham Hall Press.

Singletary, Harry K., Jr. 1993. "Suggestions." Tallahassee, Fla., Florida Department of Corrections. Unpublished document.

South Carolina Department of Corrections. 1992. *Employee/Inmate Relations: The Fine Line.* Columbia, S.C.: South Carolina Department of Corrections. Videotape.

Sue, D. W. and D. Sue. 1990. *Counseling the Culturally Different.* New York: John Wiley and Sons.

Sykes, G. and S. L. Messinger. "The inmate social code." Topeka, Kan.: Kansas Department of Corrections. Unpublished paper.

Texas Department of Criminal Justice. n.d. *New Employee Information Packet.* Huntsville, Tex.: Texas Department of Corrections.

U.S. Department of Justice. 1990. *Sourcebook of Criminal Justice Statistics—1989.* Washington, D.C.: U.S. Government Printing Office.

——. August 1991. *Drugs and Jail Inmates, 1989.* Washington, D.C.

——. 1991. *Drugs and Crime Facts, 1990.* Washington, D.C.

——. 1992. *Bureau of Justice Statistics National Update 2, no. 1.* Washington, D.C.

——. March 1992. *Women in Jail 1989.* Washington, D.C.

——. May 1992. *Prisoners in 1991.* Washington, D.C.

——. June 1992. *Jail Inmates 1991.* Washington, D.C.

——. May 1993. *Prisoners in 1992.* Washington, D.C.

——. August 1993. *Jail Inmates 1992.* Washington, D.C.

——. 1994. *Sourcebook of Criminal Justice Statistics—1993.* Washington, D.C.: U.S. Government Printing Office.

——. June 1994. *Prisoners in 1993.* Washington, D.C.

Vantour, Jim, ed. 1991. *Our Story: Organizational Renewal in Federal Corrections.* Ottawa, Ont.: Correctional Service Canada.

Virginia Criminal Code Annotated §§ 18.2-103 (1994 as amended). "Concealing or taking possession of merchandise; altering price tags; transferring goods from one container to another; counseling, etc., another in performance of such acts."

Washington State Department of Corrections. n.d. *Community Involvement Program Volunteer Handbook.* Olympia, Wash.

——. n.d. *Employee Handbook.* Olympia, Wash.

Welo, B. 1995. *Life Beyond Loss: A Workbook for Incarcerated Men.* Laurel, Md.: American Correctional Association.

Whitney, J. 1936. *Elizabeth Fry: Quaker Heroine.* Boston, Mass.: Little, Brown, and Co.

Whittaker, R. "Manning a women's prison—One officer's viewpoint." *Corrections Today* 52 (7): 158 (1990).

Wisconsin Department of Corrections. 1992. *Dodge Correctional Institution Volunteer Handbook.* Wauppun, Wis.

Wyoming Women's Center. n.d. *Wyoming Visitor's Center Visitor's Guide.* Lusk, Wy.

Yochelson, S. 1977. "The change process." *The Criminal Personality.* Vol. 2. New York: Jason Aronson.

——. 1986. "The drug user." *The Criminal Personality.* Vol. 3. Northvale, N.J.: Jason Aronson.

Yochelson, S. and S. E. Samenow. 1976. "A profile for change." *The Criminal Personality.* Vol. 1. New York: Jason Aronson.

About the Author

Daniel J. Bayse, Ed.S., has over seventeen years of experience working with corrections. He is the founder and executive director of the nonprofit Prison Family Foundation, Inc., in Auburn, Alabama.

For more than ten years, Bayse served as a member of the Virginia State Police. As part of his duties he frequently investigated crimes occurring inside Virginia prisons and helped to quell at least four riots and/or disturbances during those years. Since 1988, Bayse has provided thousands of hours in volunteer service to the Alabama and other prison systems providing training, consultation and family-based rehabilitation programs. To date, correctional authorities in twenty-nine states and four countries have used him and the foundation as a source of family-based rehabilitation programs, consultation, and/or training for staff members and volunteers.

Bayse is a licensed professional counselor, a certified family life educator, and an ordained Southern Baptist minister. He received a bachelor of theology degree from Florida Theological College in 1986, a master of science degree in family and child development from Auburn University in 1989, and a specialist in education degree in community agency counseling from Auburn University in 1992.

He is the author of two of the American Correctional Association's best-selling books: *As Free As An Eagle: The Inmate's Family Survival Guide* (1991) and *Helping Hands: A Handbook for Volunteers in Prisons and Jails* (1993).

Bayse is a member of the American Correctional Association, the National Council on Family Relations, the Family and Corrections Network, the American Counselors Association, the International Association of Addiction and Offender Counselors, and the International Association of Marriage and Family Counselors.

✒Also by Ⓓan Ⓑayse

As Free As An Eagle

A survival guide for inmates and their families. Written in easy-to-understand language, it examines the complex issues and problems families must cope with during incarceration and after release. This self-help guide teaches the offender how to establish productive relationships, develop problem-solving skills, and re-enter society on release. (1991, 235 pages)

#211-DB / Nonmembers $16.75 / ACA members $13.40

Helping Hands: A Handbook for Volunteers in Prisons and Jails

A practical guide for volunteers in correctional settings. The criminal justice system, reasons for crime, security issues, understanding the criminal personality, communicating with inmates, preventing manipulation, and inmate slang are discussed. (1993, 78 pages)

#497-DB / Nonmembers $8.40 / ACA members $6.00

✒Recommended Reading

Stressed Out! Strategies for Living and Working With Stress in Corrections

Gary F. Cornelius

Specifically designed for correctional professionals who are interested in leading healthier and more productive lives. Identifies what stress is and teaches strategies on how to combat it both on and off the job through such techniques as time management, relaxation, diet, and exercise. Describes how the offender subculture and offender manipulation can be the cause of stress and what workers can do to prevent it. Also teaches ways supervisors can help their subordinates cope with stress. (1994, 138 pages)

#257-DB / Nonmembers $21.95 / ACA members $17.50

The Effective Correctional Officer

Thought-provoking essays address the interests and concerns of the correctional officer. Each chapter is written by a seasoned corrections professional who speaks from first-hand knowledge and experience. Topics discussed include ethics, stress management, cross-cultural supervision, hostage situations, inmate management, litigation, substance abuse, and career growth. Excellent reading for both the novice and veteran line officer. (1992, 112 pages)

#216-DB / Nonmembers $18.00 / ACA members $14.40

Life Beyond Loss: A Workbook For Incarcerated Men

Beverly K. Welo

A proven, effective program that allows incarcerated men to examine their feelings and how they have dealt with issues of pain and loss in their lives. The workbook exercises teach offenders how to resolve their feelings in a positive manner and stop the cycle of negative choices that led to their incarceration. Issues discussed include death and loss, the cycle of grief, pain avoidance and substance abuse, grief and incarceration, denial and protest, acceptance, and resolution. (1995, 77 pages)

#347-DB / Nonmembers $12.00 / ACA members $9.60

Correctional Officer Resource Guide

An essential reference manual on all aspects of a correctional officer's job. This excellent training tool covers topics such as officers' legal liabilities, inmate programming, security, AIDS and other health issues, use of firearms, segregation, methods of restraining inmates, emergency procedures, officer support programs, and contraband. (1989, 140 pages)

#130-DB / Nonmembers $20.95 / ACA members $16.75

 To order any of these titles or to request a free publications catalog, call 1-800-825-2665.